ASIAN DELIGHTS
All~Time Favourite Recipes

Betty Yew

TIMES BOOKS INTERNATIONAL
Singapore • Kuala Lumpur

Cover photography by Ho Khee Tong of Twinlens Studio.
Photography on pages 1, 4, 7, 8, 10, 15, 16, 52, 53, 82, 83, 94, 100,
102, 103, 107, 08, 111, 112, 113, 114, 127, 148, 149, 156, 157, 164,
178, 129, 184, 198, 200, 201, 210 and 218 by Yim Chee Peng of
Culinary Studios, with food styling by Judy Chang.
Photography on pages ii, iii, iv, viii, ix, x, xi, xii, xiii, xiv and xv
by Tuck Loong.
Additional photography by Dewa bin Othman, Yew Foo
Weng and Harold Teo.

Illustrations by Agnes Tan See Mui and Anuar Abdul Rahim.

Crockery for cover courtesy of Tangs.
Crockery courtesy of Metro, Parjkson Grand, Yaohan of
Malaysia; Indian utensils on pages 148, 149 and 198 courtesy
of Uma Pushpanathan, Shymala Balashandran and Susie Ng;
silver tea set on pages 82 and oil lamps on pages 178 courtesy
of Michael Tay.

First published 1989
Reprinted 1992, 1994

© 1989 TIMES EDITIONS PTE LTD
Published by Times Books International
an imprint of Times Editions Pte Ltd

Times Centre, 1 New Industrial Road, Singapore 1953

Times Subang, Lot 46 Subang Hi-Tech Industrial Park
Batu Tiga, 40000 Shah Alam, Selangor Darul Ehsan, Malaysia.

Printed in Singapore

ISBN 981 204 359 4

For my parents

Contents

Preface

This book should delight those who are in a festive mood or seek something different as this underlies my selection of recipes for this book. Readers will find all they need to know about how to make the delicacies the Chinese serve during the Lunar New Year, the delights of the Malays for Hari Raya and the Deepavali sensations of the Indians. I have also included the most popular items served in Malay, Chinese, Indian and Eurasian homes and in the ubiquitous food stalls which make up our gourmet's paradise.

In a nutshell, this book graphically details the food culture of the different ethnic groups in Malaysia and Singapore with snippets of information on the festivals and customs associated with the various foods featured.

I first ventured into writing food books partly to help cement the bond of friendship. The publications of my previous three books – *Asian High Tea*, *Time For Dessert* and *Rasa Malaysia* – brought new friends and new demands – demands for 'more of the same'. I hope that with this new book, others will share with their friends a new adventure in culinary experiences and hopefully some will be invited for 'more of the same'.

This book would not have been possible without the help of a whole host of people who helped source, buy, chop, slice, grind and taste the hundreds of recipes found in this collection. In particular I would like to thank Soh Chak Yuen, Choo Ee, Evelyn Eu, Gweneth Ruth Scholeman, Molly Tan, Sue Teo, Devi, Winnie Tan, V. Lakhiani and Asha M. Devanani.

My final wish – 'Towards better friendship with common appreciation in tastes.' HAPPY COOKING!

Betty Tan
August 1989

Weights and Measures

All the recipes in this book have been tested with metric measures. I've chosen to use these measurements as they are more convenient and easier to use. But for those not yet familiar with these, imperial units of mass, length, volume and cooking temperatures are given here. Liquid measurements are given using a metric cup (standard 250 ml). However, these do not have to be adhered to precisely as different cookers vary in heat intensity. A little extra liquid can be added, for instance, if meat is not properly cooked. Quantities for salt and sugar can be varied to suit individual tastes.

I've also chosen to use Australian measuring spoons (1 tablespoon = 20 ml). Cooks using British and American measuring spoons should vary the quantities specified slightly (British tablespoon = 17.7 ml; American tablespoon = 15 ml). All spoon measurements given are level unless otherwise stated.

(All measurements given are approximations only.)

Mass

30 g	1 oz	**390 g**	13 oz
60 g	2 oz	**420 g**	14 oz
90 g	3 oz	**450 g**	15 oz
120 g	4 oz	**480 g**	16 oz (1 lb)
150 g	5 oz	**500 g**	1 lb ⅔ oz
180 g	6 oz	**600 g**	1 lb 4 oz (1¼ lb)
210 g	7 oz	**720 g**	1 lb 8 oz (1½ lb)
240 g	8 oz	**840 g**	1 lb 12 oz (1¾ lb)
250 g	8⅓ oz	**960 g**	2 lb
270 g	9 oz	**1 kg**	2 lb 1⅓ oz
300 g	10 oz	**1.2 kg**	2 lb 8 oz (2½ lb)
330 g	11 oz	**1.5 kg**	3 lb 2 oz (3⅛ lb)
360 g	12 oz	**2 kg**	4 lb 2⅔ oz

Length/Width

2.5 cm	1 in
5 cm	2 in
7.5 cm	3 in
10 cm	4 in
12.5 cm	5 in
15 cm	6 in
20 cm	8 in
25 cm	10 in
30 cm	12 in (1 ft)

Volume

30 ml	1 fl oz
120 ml	4 fl oz
240 ml	8 fl oz
480 ml	16 fl oz

Cup Equivalents

1 cup liquid	250 ml	(6 tablespoons liquid = ½ cup)
		(12 tablespoons liquid = 1 cup)
2 cups liquid	500 ml	
1 cup flour	120 g	4 oz (1 tablespoon flour = 30 g/1 oz)
1 cup sugar/rice	240 g	8 oz (1 rounded tablespoon sugar = 30 g/1 oz)

Oven Temperatures

This again is only an approximate guide. Different makes of ovens vary and even the same make of oven can give slightly different individual results at the same temperature. Thus, it is impossible to be exact for every oven, but the following is a good guide. If in doubt, refer to your oven manual's temperature chart. Always preheat the oven 15 minutes before use.

Description of oven temperature	°C	°F	Gas Regulo
Cool	150	300	4
	160	325	5
Moderate	175	350	6
Moderately hot	190	375	7
Hot	205	400	8
Very hot	220	425	9

List of Recipes

Chinese Snacks

List of Recipes

Dim Sum

List of Recipes

Malay Delights

Kuih-Muih

List of Recipes

List of Recipes

Indian Fare

List of Recipes

Sugar and Spice

Cakes and Bakes

List of Recipes

List of Recipes

Kong Hee Fatt Choy!

The Chinese or Lunar New Year marks the beginning of spring, an important event for the originally agricultural people. Now, whether living in modern cities or tiny villages, Chinese all over the world celebrate this most important festival in the Chinese calendar, which begins on the first day of the twelfth moon and lasts for 15 days. This is a time of family reunion and of preparation for a luckier and more prosperous year ahead. There is always a frantic rush shopping for all kinds of seasonal delicacies for the New Year, mandarin oranges for good luck and flowers and kumquat trees to beautify homes. The year must begin with a clean slate – all debts are settled, the house is spring cleaned and everyone must have new clothes. Red is the dominant colour as it is believed that this is the colour that evil fears. During the 15 days, it is traditional to visit family and friends, renewing kinship bonds with *ang pows* (red packets containing money) being distributed to unmarried persons, be they six or sixty, as a token of good luck.

Even the food served is significant for the New Year – candies sweeten one's fate, mandarin oranges are symbolic of wealth and glutinous cakes ensure good fortune.

Food to ensure a good year ahead: (top tray) *Nian Kao* (p 4) surrounded by kumquats, red dates, preserved melon, dried longans, white and red melon seeds and peanuts; (tray on right, clockwise from top) Almond Butter Crisps (p 226), *Luk Tow Peang* (p 9), Sesame Glutinous Balls with Bean Paste and Peanut Fillings (p 6), Sweet Glutinous Bean Paste Rolls (p 5), Kuih Bangkit (p 136), *Nian Kao* with Yam (p 4), Dainty Pineapple Tarts (p 230) and (centre) *Long Yok Korn* (p 2); (tray on left, clockwise from top) Golden Fruit Cake (p 207), Traditional Sugee Cake (p 203), *Kuih Kapit* (p 137) and Pineapple-Shaped Tarts (p 231); and (foreground) Red Date Tea (p 7).

Long Yok Korn
(Dried Sweet Meat)

A great favourite during the Chinese New Year, this can be bought from the numerous stalls that sell it during the season, and all year round. But if you can't get it and desperately need to have some, try this easy enough recipe. Some of the ingredients may be difficult to find, but believe me, the result is worth the effort.

Preparation: 1 hour
Grilling: 30 minutes
Net weight after grilling: 1¹/₄ kg

2 kg pork chop or pork loin
1¹/₂ teaspoons bicarbonate of soda
1 square piece fermented bean curd (lam yee)
1¹/₂ teaspoons five spice powder
3 teaspoons salt
750 g rock sugar, crushed
6 tablespoons light soya suace
3 tablespoons fish sauce
1¹/₂ tablespoons rice wine
1¹/₂ teaspoons red colouring
6 tablespoons oil

Fermented bean curd (lam yee)
Sold in jars, these are cubes of preserved soft beancurd soaked in a solution of brine, wine and chillies. It has a very strong flavour and the Chinese like to eat it with white rice porridge. Also known as preserved beancurd or Chinese cheese.

Wash and dry meat thoroughly. Partially freeze meat to facilitate cutting. Cut into thin slices and marinate with remaining ingredients. Leave to steep in seasonings overnight in the refrigerator.

Next day, place meat slices in lightly oiled baking trays and dry in the sun for 3 hours. Turn meat slices over after the first 1¹/₂ hours. If bigger pieces of meat are preferred, join slices of meat by overlapping the edges. After drying, cut the meat into required sizes.

Grill over smouldering charcoal for a minute on each side or until lightly browned and fragrant.

Grandma's Prawn Crackers

Another snack that's served at Chinese New Year which is easily bought but more fun home-made, and tastier too.

Preparation: 1 hour
Cooking: 1 hour
Makes: 120 pieces

600 g prawns, shelled and deveined
1 egg
1 tablespoon salt
1 tablespoon sugar
600 g tapioca flour
½ cup water

Grind prawns to a fine paste. Beat in egg. Add salt and sugar and beat mixture thoroughly. Sift in tapioca flour and knead well. Add water and again knead well.

Form into 3 rolls and place in a steamer. Cover rolls with a dry cloth to prevent water from dripping onto the rolls. Steam for 1 hour. When rolls are cooked, cool and refrigerate overnight, then cut rolls into thin slices. Dry in the sun.

When throughly dried, store prawn crackers in an air-tight container ready for deep frying.

Nian Kao
with Yam/Sweet Potato

Preparation: 20 minutes
Frying: 15 minutes

45 g plain flour
45 g rice flour
1 cup water
1 teaspoon baking powder
¼ teaspoon salt

24 pieces
(¼ cm x 5 cm x 4 cm)
nian kao
12 pieces yam/sweet potato, same size as *nian kao*

oil for deep frying

Sift plain and rice flours into a mixing bowl. Add water and mix to a smooth batter. Stir in baking powder and salt.

Sandwich a piece of yam in between two pieces of *nian kao*. Dip into batter and carefully drop into hot oil. Reduce heat a little and fry for approximately 12-15 minutes until light golden brown on both sides.

Dessicated coconut or pineapple ring tins can be used if small cake tins are not available.

Nian Kao
(Sweet New Year Cake)

The days before the Chinese New Year are frantic with all kinds of preparation. Besides the cooking of New Year goodies, special rituals also have to be done for the household gods, particularly *Tsao Wang*, the Kitchen God who departs on an annual trip to Heaven to report on the family's conduct during the past year. *Nian kao* is offered to *Tsao Wang* to ensure that he makes 'sweet' reports of the family. And while he is away, his image kept in the kitchen is turned to face the wall.

You may not follow this practice, but that shouldn't stop you from trying this ancient Chinese cake. Here's a simplified version of the original recipe and a variation that I'm sure you'll enjoy. And you don't have to eat it just at the festival period – *nian kao* keeps well in the refrigerator for at least a year.

Preparation: 15 minutes
Cooking: 9 hours

300 g glutinous rice flour
1 cup water
300 g sugar
banana leaves, cut into 6 cm strips and scalded

Line two 9 cm round cake tins with banana leaves. The banana leaves should be 5 cm higher than the cake tins. Fold over the edges of the cake tin and tie with a piece of string or rubber band.

Sift glutinous rice flour into a mixing bowl. Pour in water and mix well. Add sugar and mix by hand or with a wooden spoon until sugar completely dissolves. Pour batter into the prepared tins and place in a steamer. Steam over rapidly boiling water for 1 hour. Remove the cover. Dip a spoon into some cooking oil and lightly oil and smooth the cake surface with the back of the spoon. Cover the tins with 3 layers of newspapers to prevent water from dripping onto the cake surface. Reduce heat to moderate and steam for 9 hours. Maintain water level in the steamer by constantly adding boiling water. When done, cake will turn a caramel brown. Leave in tin to cool for 24 hours before removing.

Sweet Glutinous Bean Paste Roll

Preparation: 30 minutes
Cooking: 25 minutes

480 g glutinous rice, soaked for 3 hours and drained
1 cup thick coconut milk and 1 cup thin coconut milk ,
from 1 grated white coconut
¼ teaspoon salt
2 tablespoons sugar
1 dessertspoon cornoil
5 tablespoons roasted sesame seeds, approximate

210 g prepared sweet bean paste filling
(see recipe for ham chin peng *on p 49)*

Put glutinous rice in a 20 cm cake pan. Stir in thin coconut milk, salt sugar and cornoil. Steam over rapidly boiling water for 15 minutes. Pour thick coconut milk over rice and steam for a further 10 minutes. Remove and cool a little.

Sprinkle sesame seeds on a piece of muslin cloth. Carefully spread and press the cooked glutinous rice over the sesame seeds to a rectangle about 1 cm in thickness. To ensure even thickness place a plastic sheet on the spread-out rice and carefully roll out to flatten with a rolling pin. Spread with a layer of sweet bean paste filling (or sambal *udang kering*).

From the two ends, roll each end toward the centre with the help of the muslin cloth to form two joined swiss rolls. Wrap the glutinous roll with the muslin cloth and refrigerate until cold. Carefully unwrap and cut into 2 cm slices.

Sambal Udang Kering (Dried Prawn Sambal)

This delicious filling is wonderful as a savoury or sandwich filling, or served with porridge or rice.

A
300 g dried prawns, rinsed and drained
12 shallots
4 cloves garlic
15 fresh red chillies

6 tablespoons cooking oil
1 teaspoonful sugar
¼ teaspoon salt

Pound **A** with a mortar and pestle or blend until fine in an electric mincer.

Heat oil in a *kuali* until hot. Add ground ingredients reduce heat and stir fry for 20-30 minutes until *sambal* is reddish-brown, fragrant and quite dry. Add the sugar and salt and mix well. Dish out to cool completely and store in an air-tight container. Use as required. Keeps well in the refrigerator for at least a month.

Peanut Filling

100 g peanuts, roasted and coarsely ground
100 g granulated sugar

Combine roasted peanuts and sugar in a bowl and leave aside. Use as required.

(To roast raw peanuts, spread them out in a tray and bake on the top shelf of a very hot oven, stirring from time to time, until golden brown or pan-fry over low heat, stirring constantly until golden brown. Rub the thin brown skin off, then winnow in a flat tray or basket. After cooling, grind coarsely in an electric chopper for a few seconds. Ground peanuts can be frozen and kept for 3-4 months.)

Bean Paste Filling

250 g prepared bean paste (see *ham chin peng* filling on p 49)

Divide bean paste into 12 equal portions and shape each into a round ball approximately 20 g in weight. Use as required.

Sesame Glutinous Balls with Peanut Filling and Bean Paste Filling

Sweet cakes with two different fillings that are served for Chinese New Year.

Preparation: 30 minutes
Cooking: 15 minutes
Makes: 12

75 g sesame seeds
300 g glutinous rice flour
150 g sweet potato, boiled and mashed
3½ tablespoons sugar
⅔ cup water, approximate

Wash sesame seeds in a deep bowl of water. Pour sesame seeds, stirring water at the same time, into a sieve. This way, the heavier grit and sand will remain at the bottom of the bowl.

Sift glutinous rice flour onto a board. Make a well in the centre, add mashed sweet potato, sugar and water. Using fingertips, mix and work with flour to form a firm ball of dough. Add a little extra water, if necessary. Knead for 5-10 minutes until dough is firm, pliable and smooth but not sticky. Form into a long roll and cut into 12 equal portions, each approximately 60 g in weight. Shape these into small balls.

Flatten each ball into a round about 7½ cm in diameter. Put in one dessertspoonful of filling in the centre and gather edges to enclose filling. Pinch firmly to seal and then shape into a round ball. Moisten balls with wet hands and toss in sesame seeds.

Deep fry over medium heat, half a dozen at a time, for 5 minutes until golden brown. Remove with perforated ladle and place on absorbent paper.

Pie Tee (Top Hats)

Great idea for a brunch or tea party which is also served at Chinese New Year. Everything can be prepared in advance – just sit back and relax, watching your guests enjoy themselves making these little 'top hats'. The special moulds used can be found in night markets or department stores.

Preparation: 1 hour
Cooking: 1½ hours
Makes: 38

90 g plain flour
1 tablespoon rice flour
¼ teaspoon salt
1 egg, beaten
¾ cup water
oil for deep frying
3 tablespoons oil
4 cloves garlic, minced
450 g turnip (bangkwang), finely shredded and squeezed to get rid of a little water
240 g chicken or pork, diced
240 g prawns, diced
A
¼ teaspoon five spice powder
1 teaspoon salt
¼ teaspoon pepper
90 g crabmeat
1 bunch local lettuce for lining pie tee shells
finely sliced crispy shallots
coriander leaves

Sift plain and rice flours into a small bowl. Add salt. Stir in egg and mix with water to make a smooth runny batter. Strain if batter is lumpy.

Heat oil in a deep pan and heat *pie tee* mould in hot oil for a minute. Remove hot mould and dip in batter. Place mould in hot oil till *pie tee* is golden in colour. Loosen and drain on absorbent paper. When cool, store in an air-tight tin till required.

Red Date Tea

Red Date Tea is served to guests during Chinese New Year as it symbolizes luck, prosperity and wealth.

Preparation: 5 minutes
Boiling: 40 minutes
Makes: 4 tea cups

120 g Chinese red dates, rinsed
180 g sugar
4 cups water
15 g dried longan (without shell), rinsed

Put all ingredients in a saucepan and bring to a boil. Reduce heat and simmer for 30 minutes until fragrant.

(cont'd on p 8)

Heat oil in a *kuali* and lightly brown minced garlic. Add turnip and stir fry, then add chicken and prawns. Add **A** and stir in crabmeat. Simmer till quite dry, then dish up and cool.

To serve, line *pie tee* shell with a small piece of lettuce. Put in 2 teaspoons filling and garnish with crispy shallots and coriander leaves. Serve with chilli sauce.

Luk Tow Koh (Green Bean Cake)

A cross between a cookie and a cake – really!

Press the mixture for *Luk Tow Peang* into a larger but flatter mould. Tap out the cookies/cakes and put onto a steamer tray lined with a muslin cloth. Steam over rapidly boiling water for 5 minutes. Cover the steamer tray with a cloth to ensure that water from the cover does not drip onto the cookies/cakes.

Luk Tow Peang (Green Bean Cookie)

A Cantonese favourite for the Chinese New Year.

Preparation: 45 minutes
Baking: 30 minutes
Oven setting: 165 ℃
Makes: 80-100

250 g mung/green beans, washed, drained and dried in the sun
120 g castor sugar
¼ cup water

Pan-fry the green beans for 10 minutes over low heat. Cool and grind in an electric blender until very fine. (For really fragrant green bean cookies, it is preferable to grind freshly roasted beans.)

Sift the green bean flour into a mixing bowl. There should be about 240 g of the sifted ground beans. Stir in castor sugar. Sprinkle the water, a little at a time and carefully stir into the flour mixture with the hand. Mixture should resemble find breadcrumbs and it should be able to hold its shape when pressed into a lump.

Take a handful of crumbly bean mixture and fill a special wooden green bean mould (p 15). Press firmly. Level and scrape off excess mixture with a knife. Tap out the imprinted cookies lightly.

Place on ungreased cookie tray. Dry for 1 week in the hot sun until cookies turn a little whitish. Alternatively, cookies can be baked in very low oven for 8 hours or until they turn whitish. Cool and store in an air-tight container.

Tung Ying
(Sweet Glutinous Rice Balls)

Tung Ying is eaten as a symbol of union on *Tung Chih* which falls on the fifth day of the eleventh moon. Coincidently, this always seems to fall just two days before Christmas Day.

Preparation: 45 minutes
Cooking: 20 minutes

A
5 cups water
500 g sugar
5 pandan leaves, knotted
1 packet (600 g) glutinous rice flour
2 cups water, approximate
a few drops yellow colouring
a few drops red colouring
a few drops blue colouring
a few drops green colouring
1 teaspoon pandan juice

Put **A** into a pot and bring to a boil. Remove when sugar completely dissolves. Allow syrup to cool.

Sift glutinous rice flour into a bowl and mix into a firm stiff dough with water. Place dough on a board and knead well for 10 minutes. Divide dough into two equal portions. Keep one half of the dough for white glutinous balls. Divide remaining half into 4 smaller equal portions. Knead each portion separately adding a few drops of the different colouring. Add pandan juice into the green coloured portion.

Roll each portion of dough starting with the white dough into a long roll and break into small even pieces. Roll each firmly into the size of a marble ball. Place rice balls on a clean dish cloth. This will absorb a little moisture from the rice balls. Repeat procedure with the yellow, red, blue and green dough. Wash hands each time you roll a different colour to prevent discolouring.

Bring half a saucepan of water to a boil. Put in white rice balls and cook a couple of minutes until they rise to the surface. Remove with a perforated ladle and drop them into a bowl of cool water. Repeat with the yellow, red, blue and green coloured rice balls.

Drain thoroughly the cooked rice balls and place in cooled syrup. Serve in individual bowls.

Breakfast in high style:
(from left to right) *Nyonya Chang* (p 11),
Kee Chang served with sugar (p 14), *Bak
Chang* (p 12) *Tow Suan* served with *You
Tiau* (p 47 & 48) and *Ang Koo* (p 15).

Changs (Rice Dumplings)

These rice dumplings wrapped in bamboo leaves are made for the Dragon Boat Festival which falls on the fifth day of the fifth moon of the lunar calendar. Legend has it that *Chao Yuen*, a Minister of the State of Chu, committed suicide by drowning himself in a river in protest because his King didn't accept his advice. The people, realising his loyalty after his death, went in search of his body in the river. This developed into the Dragon Boat Festival, and rice dumplings, wrapped in bamboo leaves and tied with five-coloured silk threads, were thrown into the river for *Chao Yuen's* departed soul.

The dumplings remain very much the same – glutinous rice with meat fillings (there are two different recipes here) and still wrapped in bamboo leaves but only tied with ordinary fibrous strings today.

Nyonya Chang

An age-old Peranakan recipe that is a mixture of sweet and savoury.

Preparation: 1 hour
Cooking: 40 minutes
Steaming: 2 hours
Makes: 22 *chang*

1 kg glutinous rice
44 bamboo or chang *leaves, trim 2 cm off both ends*
1 tablespoon alkaline water
60 g dried chestnuts, soaked for 1 hour
6 dried Chinese mushrooms, soaked until soft, drained and finely diced
½ teaspoon sugar
1 teaspoon light soya sauce
300 g lean pork, finely diced
1 tablespoon coriander powder, roasted
½ cup cooking oil
180 g shallots and 3 cloves garlic, sliced
90 g preserved winter melon, finely diced
1 teaspoon salt
1 teaspoonful dark soya sauce
¼ cup oil
2 teaspoons salt
1 tablespoonful shallot crisps
22 pieces dried China grass, soaked, or string

Bamboo/*chang* leaves
These can be bought from Chinese provision stores and from supermarkets during *chang* festival times. Boiling them with a little alkaline water will prevent the *chang* from sticking to the leaves. To ensure that you have enough to wrap all the glutinous rice, boil additional leaves and if there are holes in the bamboo leaves, use two instead of one.

(cont'd on p 12)

1

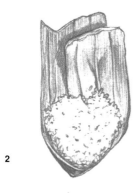

2

3

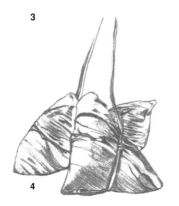

4

Wash and soak glutinous rice for 8 hours. Wash the bamboo leaves and place in a large pot of water with alkaline water and boil for 5 minutes. Drain.

Boil chestnuts for 15-20 minutes until soft. Split into two. Season mushrooms with sugar and light soya sauce. Combine pork and mushrooms with coriander powder.

Heat ½ cup of oil in a *kuali* and brown shallots and garlic. Add pork mixture, chestnuts, preserved winter melon and fry for 2 minutes. Mix in salt and dark soya sauce. Leave aside.

Heat ¼ cup of oil and fry glutinous rice for 3-5 minutes with salt. Dish out and mix in shallot crisps.

Take two pieces of bamboo leaves, place back to back and adjust to required lengths. Shape the leaves like a cone. Place and spread 1 tablespoon of rice in the cone. Put in 1 tablespoon of the filling and top with 1½-2 tablespoons of rice. Wrap and tie securely with dried China grass or string.

Bring a large pot of water (enough to cover *chang*) to a boil. Put in *chang* and boil for 2 hours. Top constantly with boiling water to maintain level of water. Remove when cooked and hang *chang* to dry.

Bak Chang
(Meat Dumplings)

Preparation: 40 minutes
Cooking: 15 minutes
Makes: 24

1½ *kg glutinous rice*
50 *bamboo or* chang *leaves*
1 *tablespoon alkaline water*
600 *g belly pork, cut into 1 cm x 3 cm pieces*

A
4 teaspoons sugar
2 teaspoonfuls pepper
2 teaspoons five spice powder
2 teaspoons salt
4 teaspoons sesame oil
4 teaspoons oyster sauce
4 teaspoons dark soya sauce

60 g dried chestnuts, soaked for 1 hour
6 dried Chinese mushrooms, soaked, drained and quartered
½ teaspoon sugar
½ cup oil
30 g dried prawns, soaked and drained
60 g shallots and 1 whole pod garlic, sliced
½ teaspoon salt

2 tablespoons oil
4 cloves garlic, chopped
2 teaspoons salt
¾ teaspoon five spice powder
2 teaspoonfuls dark soya sauce

25 pieces dried China grass, soaked for 5 minutes or string

Wash and soak rice for 8 hours. Wash and boil the *chang* leaves in a large cooking pot with alkaline water for 5 minutes. Drain.

Season pork with **A** for 30 minutes. Boil chestnuts for 15-20 minutes until soft. Drain and split into two. Leave aside.

Season mushrooms with sugar. Heat ½ cup oil and fry mushrooms for 2 minutes. Drain and leave aside. Add dried prawns and stir fry for 1 minute. Drain and leave aside. Add shallots and garlic and fry until golden brown and fragrant. Add seasoned pork, salt and stir fry for 2 minutes only. Pork should be half-cooked. Remove and leave aside.

Heat 2 tablespoons of oil and brown garlic. Add rice, salt, five spice powder and dark soya sauce. Fry for 5 minutes more. Dish out.

Dried china grass
From China, these are mainly used for tying *chang*s and rice wrapped in lotus leaves.

(cont'd on p 14)

For wrapping the *chang*, take two pieces of *chang* leaves. Place back to back and adjust the lengths. Fold into a cone shape. Place and spread 1 tablespoon of rice in the cone. Put in 1 piece of mushroom, 2-3 pieces of dried prawns, 2-3 pieces of chestnuts and 1 tablespoon of pork. Cover filling with 1 tablespoon of rice. Wrap into a tight cone and bind securely with dried China grass or string.

Tie all the wrapped *chang* into two bunches. Bring a large pot of water to a boil. Put in *chang* and cook for 2 hours. Top constantly with boiling water to maintain level of water at all times. Remove and hang *chang* to dry.

Kee Chang
(Alkaline Dumplings)

This rice dumpling doesn't have a meat filling but is served with syrup.

Preparation: 10 minutes
Cooking: 5 hours
Makes: 21-22 *chang*

600 g glutinous rice
2 dessertspoons alkaline water
¼ teaspoon borax (pangsar) *(this is used to improve the texture of glutinous rice to make it 'springy')*

21-22 bamboo or chang *leaves*
1 tablespoon alkaline water
22 pieces dried China grass or string

Palm Sugar Syrup

A
180 g *gula melaka* (palm sugar), chopped
1 tablespoon sugar
½ cup water

Boil A until sugar dissolves. Strain.

Wash and soak glutinous rice for at least 10 hours. Drain well. Stir in alkaline water and borax with the rice.

To wrap *chang*, take a piece of bamboo leaf, fold into a cone shape. Put in 1 tablespoon of glutinous rice. Wrap into a cone and bind securely with dried China grass or string. (*Kee chang* is usually much smaller than *bak* or *nonya chang*.) Knot all the *chang* into two bunches.

Bring a large pot of water to a boil. Ensure there is enough water to cover *chang*. Put in the two bunches and boil for 5 hours. Top constantly with boiling water to maintain the level of water at all times. Remove and hang to dry.

Serve *kee chang* with palm sugar syrup.

Ang Koo (Red Cake)

Symbolising longevity, luck and prosperity, this is distributed during birthday celebrations of the elderly and after the one-month celebration of newborn babies. Here are 2 recipes, the one without coconut milk will keep longer and better but the coconut milk used in the second recipe gives the pastry a delicate coconut flavour. There are also two recipes for the mung bean filling with the second one being easier.

Preparation: 1 hour
Cooking: 15 minutes
Steaming: 2 hours
Makes: 34

600 g glutinous rice flour
180 g granulated sugar
½ cup cornoil
1½ cups boiling hot water
few drops red colouring
few drops yellow colouring
banana leaves, trimmed into 7.5 cm rounds

Sift glutinous rice flour into a large mixing bowl. Put 2 tablespoons of the sifted flour into a small piece of muslin cloth and tie up securely with a piece of string. Use this for dusting the *ang koo* mould.

Add sugar to glutinous rice flour. Make a well in the centre and add cornoil, hot water and red and yellow colourings. Knead well until colouring is even and dough turns glossy. Form dough into rounds, slightly larger than the size of a golf ball. Flatten each ball slightly to hold a ball of sweet bean filling. Pinch and seal the edges to form a round ball.

Lightly dust *ang koo* mould with the bag of glutinous rice flour. Press the round ball of dough into the mould, tap mould lightly on the surface of table to remove *ang koo*. Place on greased banana leaves. Carefully brush with cornoil and steam over rapidly boiling water for 20 minutes.

Moulds for Chinese cakes: (top tp bottom) Moon Cake (p 16), *Ang Koo* (p 15) and *Luk Tow Peang* (p 8).

Mung Bean Filling (1)

1 kg skinned mung/green beans, washed and soaked overnight
³/₄ cup water
4 pandan leaves, knotted
750 g sugar

Drain mung beans and steam over rapidly boiling water for 45 minutes. Mash with a potato masher whilst hot and set aside.

Put water in a *kuali* and bring to a boil. Add pandan leaves and sugar and stir over low heat till the sugar turns into syrup. Add the mashed beans, stirring continuously until mixture is almost dry (the mung beans will become a sweet yellow paste). Discard pandan leaves and leave to cool. Form sweet mung bean paste filling into golf size balls.

Ang Koo with Coconut Milk

Preparation: 1 hour
Cooking: 15 minutes
Steaming: 2 hours
Makes: 24

250 g glutinous rice flour
1 cup coconut milk, from ½ grated coconut
1½ tablespoons sugar
2 pandan leaves, knotted
2 dessertspoons cornoil
24 pieces (7.5 cm rounds) banana leaves, greased

Sift glutinous rice flour into a mixing bowl.

In a small saucepan, combine coconut milk and sugar and bring to a slow boil together with pandan leaves. Keep stirring until sugar dissolves. Add boiling coconut milk mixture to glutinous rice flour and mix well with a wooden spoon. Knead into a soft dough. Divide into 24 portions and form into round balls. Flatten each slightly, place a ball of mung bean paste in the centre, wrap and gather the edges to enclose the filling.

Press the ball of dough into a small greased *ang koo* mould to get an imprint. Tap out the *ang koo* and place on a round of banana leaf. Steam over rapidly boiling water for 3 minutes.

Mung Bean Filling (2)

500 g mung/green beans (without the skin)
3 tablespoons oil
300 g sugar

Wash and soak mung beans for at least 4 hours. Drain. Cook in a rice cooker with water reaching just below the surface of beans. Cool and grind into a fine paste without adding water.

Heat oil in a *kuali*. Add sugar and cook for 15 minutes, stirring all the time until sugar dissolves. When syrup thickens, add mung bean paste. Cook until paste is sticky. Remove and cool. Store in the refrigerator or freezer until required.

Divide mung bean paste into 24 portions. Form into round balls. Leave aside.

Moon Cake with Lotus Seed Paste and Single Egg Yolk

Chinese the world over celebrate the Moon Cake or Mid-Autumn Festival on the fifteenth day of the eigth month of the lunar calendar, with moon cakes and lanterns. In the 14th century, during the uprising against the Mogul rulers, moon cakes were used to hold secret messages. But nowadays, instead of messages, these cakes can have fillings such as black bean paste (*tau sar*), mung bean paste (*tow yong*), almond paste (*han yan*) and a mixed nuts, seeds and Chinese bacon mincemeat filling (*kum thoi*).

Here is a recipe for the most popular by far (and also quite expensive when bought) – lotus seed paste (*ling yong*). Freshly made moon cakes will have a crisp pastry which will turn a softer texture after 2-3 days and mooncakes are best when eaten a week after baking.

Preparation: 1½ hours
Cooking: 1½ hours
Baking: 25 minutes
Oven temperature: 190°C

600 g red lotus seeds with skin
water to boil
½ tablespoon alkaline water
4 cups water

600 g sugar
2½ cups peanut oil
1 tablespoon maltose (mak ngar tong)

16 salted egg yolks, steamed for 10 minutes or baked in an oven at 175°C for 5-10 minutes, and cooled

300 g golden syrup
½ cup groundnut oil
½ tablespoon alkaline water
2 tablespoons flour

480 g plain flour
1 egg, beaten

Wash lotus seeds and boil with water. When it begins to boil, add alkaline water and continue boiling for 5 minutes. Drain. Add cold water and rub off the skins till all the lotus seeds are cleaned. If using whole lotus seeds, remove the green centres. Boil the cleaned lotus seeds again with water until soft. Blend into a fine paste in an electric blender.

In a large saucepan, melt half the sugar until it turns light golden. Add the lotus seed paste and cook stirring all the time until it thickens. Add remaining sugar and peanut oil, a little at a time. Cook until thick, then stir in maltose. Keep stirring until paste leaves the sides of the saucepan. To test for doneness, cool a lump of cooked lotus seed paste and slice through with a knife. If the knife comes out clean, the paste is of the right consistency.

When cool, divide paste into 16 portions, each about 120 g in weight. Wrap each portion with a salted egg yolk and form into a round ball. Leave aside.

Moon Biscuits

For those who love the pastry without the rich filling!

Preparation: 30 minutes
Baking: 20 minutes
Oven temperature: 190°C

Divide dough for moon cake pastry into 24 portions, approximately 45 g per portion, depending on size of moon biscuit moulds. Lightly dust moulds with flour and press a portion of dough to fill mould. Tap out lightly and place on lightly greased baking trays. Brush with beaten egg and bake in hot oven until golden brown. Just 5 minutes before removing from oven, brush again with beaten egg for a glossier finish.

Golden Syrup

A good syrup should be like thick runny glue. If slightly overdone, it becomes a thick maltose consistency – just add 1-2 tablespoons of boiling water to dilute to the correct consistency. Golden syrup also improves with keeping and should be made at least 2 weeks before making moon cakes. Commercially prepared golden syrup can be used, taking the bother out of the preparation but it would cost more.

600 g sugar
1 ¾ cups water
juice of half a large lemon

Place all the ingredients in a heavy saucepan and bring to a boil. Reduce heat to low and continue boiling until syrup turns a light golden colour. Leave to cool. Keep in a storage jar at least two weeks before using.

(cont'd on p 18)

Beginners tend to use too much flour on the table. To avoid this, roll the pastry between plastic sheets, especially if the pastry is too soft. Don't worry about the thinness of the pastry, that is, as long as it doesn't crack. The pastry will rise during baking, and pastry that appears thin, barely covering the filling, will become opaque when done.

In a mixing bowl, combine golden syrup, oil and alkaline water and leave for 5 minutes. Mix in the 2 tablespoons of flour. Do not beat or knead. Leave to rest covered with a piece of dry towel for at least 3 hours, or preferably overnight at room temperature. The flour will absorb the oil more evenly if the dough is rested for longer.

Sift the rest of the flour into a mixing bowl. Make a well in the centre and pour in the syrup mixture. Slowly mix into a soft dough taking care not to knead the mixture. Divide pastry into 16 portions, each approximately 60 g in weight. (Start with more pastry dough and as you progress in experience, use up to 50 g of dough.) Flatten with the hand into a thin circular piece large enough to wrap a ball of lotus seed paste with salted egg yolk. (If you are not adept at handling the pastry, place it in between two small plastic sheets and roll out evenly to the required size.) Shape into a round ball with the filling.

Lightly dust the wooden moon cake mould (p 15) with flour. (To save time and effort, this can be done with a thin muslin bag.) Gently tap out the excess flour in the mould then press the ball of dough into the mould. Tap out lightly and place on a greased baking tray. Brush with beaten egg and bake in preheated moderate oven for 20 minutes. Remove from oven and brush again with egg glaze for a glossier finish. Return to oven and bake for a further 5 minutes or until golden brown.

Popiah

Everyone enjoys a popiah *party* whether it's at tea, lunch or brunch time. The pleased look of guests is worth all the work, and believe me, it's a lot of work!

Preparation: 2 hours (filling and garnishing)
$1\frac{1}{4}$ hours (egg skins)
Makes: approximately 48-50 medium popiahs

Filling (this may be prepared a day earlier, kept refrigerated and reheated before use)

600 g small prawns, shelled and combined with
1 teaspoon salt (reserve shells for stock)
9 cups water

7 tablespoons oil
3 whole pods garlic, minced
5 tablespoons preserved soyabeans (tau cheong), ground lightly
2 kg turnip (bangkwang), shredded
3 cans (552 g each) bamboo shoots, drained and shredded
600 g chicken meat or belly pork, cut into thin strips combined with 1 teaspoon salt

10 firm soyabean cakes, cut into strips and fried
1 teaspoon salt

Boil prawn shells in water for 5-10 minutes. Strain. Heat oil in a *kuali* and lightly brown garlic. Add preserved soyabeans and fry until fragrant. Pour in prawn stock and when it comes to a boil, add turnip and bamboo shoots. When it starts to boil again, add meat. Simmer gently for 1½ hours or transfer to a pressure cooker and pressure cook for 30 minutes. Add soyabean cakes, prawns and salt to taste and simmer for another 10 minutes.

2 heads lettuce
20 red chillies, ground
3 whole pods garlic, ground
sweet flour sauce (hak tim cheong)
600 g beansprouts, tailed and scalded
1 large cucumber, shredded finely
300 g small prawns, shelled and steamed
5 eggs, ¼ teaspoon salt, ¼ teaspoon pepper, made into thin omelettes and sliced finely
4 medium crabs, steamed and meat extracted
300 g roasted peanuts, ground
300 g shallots, sliced and fried crisp

Prepare garnishing ingredients while cooking filling. To cut preparation time, crabmeat can be extracted a day ahead and frozen. Roasted ground peanuts and shallot crisps can also be prepared well ahead and kept in air-tight containers.

To serve, put an egg skin on a plate. Place a piece of lettuce on the edge. Spread with as much fresh ground chilli, ground garlic, sweet flour sauce, beansprouts and cucumber as desired. Place 2 tablespoons of filling, drained of gravy, on top, then add a few steamed prawns, omelette strips and crabmeat. Sprinkle a little roasted ground peanuts and shallot crisps on top. Wrap and roll up like a swiss roll.

Preserved soyabeans or soyabean paste (*tau cheong*)

This dark brown, salty paste is made from fermented soyabeans, flour and salt. Available as whole beans or pureed, it's sold in jars and should be stored in the refrigerator once opened. Remember to keep the cap and neck of the jar clean. If using whole beans, mince or grind the beans according to the requirements of the recipe.

Egg Skins

10 eggs
8½ cups water
600 g flour
½ teaspoon salt

Lightly beat eggs with a fork and gradually stir in water. Sift flour into a bowl and add egg mixture gradually together with salt. Blend well and strain mixture to remove lumps. Leave for 20 minutes.

Lightly grease a 25 cm non-stick pan with a brush. Heat. To make smooth egg skins, pan has to be just hot to set skin. If it is too hot, skin will turn out perforated. Pour a ladleful of batter (about 3 tablespoons) or enough to spread over base of pan thinly, and cook over very low heat for 2 minutes or until pancake leaves sides of pan. Repeat process and stack egg skins until batter is used up.

Chinese Rojak

This Chinese salad can be prepared in advance. Toss the salad just before eating, otherwise the vegetables become very soggy.

Preparation: 20 minutes
Cooking: 10 minutes

25 dried chillies, soaked and ground
2½ cm square dried shrimp paste (belacan), toasted and ground
4 heaped tablespoons tamarind paste and
½ cup water, mixed and strained
5 tablespoons sugar
1 teaspoon dark soya sauce

1 cucumber, 2 small green mangoes, skinned,
½ medium pineapple and 300 g turnip (bangkwang),
cut into small wedges

3 teaspoons black shrimp paste (heiko)
150 g peanut candy or roasted peanuts, ground coarsely
1 tablespoon sesame seeds, roasted

Put ground ingredients and tamarind juice in a small saucepan and cook over low heat. Stir in sugar and dark soya sauce and cook until sugar dissolves and sauce is thick. Let it cool.

Mix cut vegetables with cooled sauce and black shrimp paste in large mixing bowl. Add ground peanut candy or roasted peanuts and roasted sesame seeds. Stir well and serve immediately.

Black shrimp paste (*heiko/otak udang*)
Made from shrimps, this is a thick black gluey paste with a very strong odour. It's sold in jars in Chinese provision stores and supermarkets.

Prawn Wantan Soup

You can either make your own *wantan* skins or buy the frozen variety from the supermarket.

Preparation: 20 minutes
Cooking: 10 minutes
Serves: 5 persons

6 cups fresh chicken stock (p 24), strained

A

1 tablespoon oil

1½ teaspoons salt

1 teaspoon rice wine

2 teaspoons light soya sauce

½ teaspoon sesame oil

½ teaspoon pepper

180 g small prawns, shelled and coarsely minced

45 g canned bamboo shoots, minced

B

½ teaspoon sugar

¼ teaspoon salt

¼ teaspoon pepper

1 teaspoon wine

1 teaspoon cornflour

1 stalk spring onion and 1 sprig coriander leaves, chopped

30 wantan skins

1 tablespoon oil

2 bunches mustard greens (choy sum), scalded

spring onion and coriander leaves, chopped

2 red chillies, sliced and combined with

3 tablespoons light soya sauce

Bring chicken stock and **A** to a boil. Leave aside.

Combine minced prawns and bamboo shoots and marinate with **B** for 30 minutes. Add spring onion and coriander leaves. Put a teaspoonful of prawn filling in the centre of *wantan* skin. Fold and wrap around the filling. Continue for all the filling and *wantan* skins.

Boil a saucepan of water and add oil. Drop *wantans* and cook for 1 minute. Remove with a perforated ladle and place in individual serving bowls. Use the same boiling water to scald mustard greens. Place on the sides of serving bowl.

Top with boiling soup and garnish with chopped spring onion and coriander leaves. Serve with cut chillies.

Wantan Skins

Preparation: 1 hour
Makes: 50-60 *wantan* skins

**150 g plain flour,
1 tablespoon tapioca flour,
and ⅛ teaspoon
bicarbonate of soda,
sifted together**

⅓ teaspoon salt

1 egg, lightly beaten

1½ tablespoons water

2 drops yellow colouring

Place sifted ingredients in a mixing bowl. Add rest of ingredients and knead to a soft dough.

Lightly dust table surface with tapioca flour and knead dough well. Put into a *wantan* skin roller and roll out into thin sheets or roll out with a rolling pin. Cut into required-size squares or stamp into rounds with cutters. Store in plastic wrappers or air-tight containers.

Oodles of noodles: (anticlockwise from top)
Fried Beehoon with Mixed Vegetables (p 38),
Beef shreads with Crispy Beehoon (p 34),
Fried Glass Noodles (p 24), Pork Chop Noodles in
soup (p 30), Hong Kong Styles *Sar Hor Fan* with
Beef (p 36), Hot Sour Noodles (p 31), and Dry Pork
Chop Noodles (p 29) with chilli sauce (p 33) and
sambal belacan (p 38) at left of picture.

Fried Glass Noodles

Preparation: 30 minutes
Cooking: 20 minutes
Serves: 2 persons

120 g glass noodles (tunghoon), washed and drained

A
1 teaspoon dark soya sauce
1 teaspoon light soya sauce
1 teaspoon sesame oil
1 teaspoon salt
½ teaspoon pepper

2 cups fresh chicken stock, cooled

1 chicken drumstick, deboned and cut into strips
120 g shelled medium-sized prawns

B
½ teaspoon salt
¼ teaspoon pepper
1 teaspoon light soya sauce
1 teaspoon cornflour

4 tablespoons cooking oil
3 shallots, sliced
2 cloves garlic, sliced
2 cm ginger, cut into strips

4 dried Chinese mushrooms, soaked and cut into strips
½ teaspoon light soya sauce
¼ teaspoon sesame oil
¼ teaspoon sugar

2 fresh red chillies, cut into strips
2 stalks spring onion, cut into 2 cm lengths
2 sprigs coriander leaves

Fresh chicken stock
Fresh chicken stock is the base of all good Chinese sauces and soups. Chicken cubes are really no substitute and if used, the salt to be added to the dish should be reduced according to taste.

Boil chicken bones, meat scraps, feet and giblets over low heat for half to one hour depending on the amount being made. Strain the stock before use and skim off any excess oil with a ladle. An easier way is to refrigerate the stock until the fat has set on the surface. This can be later scooped off. Excess stock, with a little salt added, can be stored in an air-tight container in the refrigerator for at least a week. You can also make fresh pork stock the same way using pork bones.

Combine **A** and add to chicken stock. Soak noodles in stock for at least 30 minutes. Season chicken and prawns with **B**.

Heat oil in *kuali* and lightly brown shallots, garlic and ginger. Add mushroom strips and stir fry. Add chicken and prawns and fry for 2 minutes. Pour in stock and *tunghoon* mixture and stir fry until liquid evaporates and mixture is almost dry.

Sprinkle chillies and spring onion and mix well. Garnish with coriander leaves. Serve hot and, if desired, with *sambal belacan* (p 38).

Tung hoon (bean thread/ transparent/glass noodles) is made from mung bean flour. The noodles are thin and transparent and when soaked look like thin glass strands, hence the name. Always soak them in stock before use. This softens and adds flavour to the otherwise bland noodle, making it much tastier.

Tasty Fried Noodles

Egg noodles are made from flour, eggs, alkaline water and yellow colouring. They are available in fine or thick strands, either fresh or dried in rolls, or dried in round cakes. Use fresh noodles for this recipe, but if they are not available, dried ones can be substituted. Just scald them a little longer – for about 2-3 minutes.

Both the fresh and dried varieties can be bought from the local market and supermarket.

Preparation: 20 minutes
Cooking: 15 minutes
Serves: 4 persons

120 g chicken or pork strips
120 g small prawns, shelled

A
½ teaspoon light soya sauce
¼ teaspoon salt
¼ teaspoon pepper

4 small rolls fresh egg noodles (wantan mee)

3 tablespoons oil
6 shallots and 5 cloves garlic, sliced
5 dried Chinese mushrooms, soaked and cut into strips
1 carrot, shredded
4 leaves Chinese cabbage (wong nga pak), *cut into strips*
300 g bean sprouts

B
2 tablespoons oyster sauce
1 tablespoon light soya sauce
1 tablespoon water
1 teaspoon dark soya sauce
1 teaspoon salt

1 stalk spring onion and 1 sprig coriander leaves, chopped
shallot crisps
1 red chilli, cut into strips

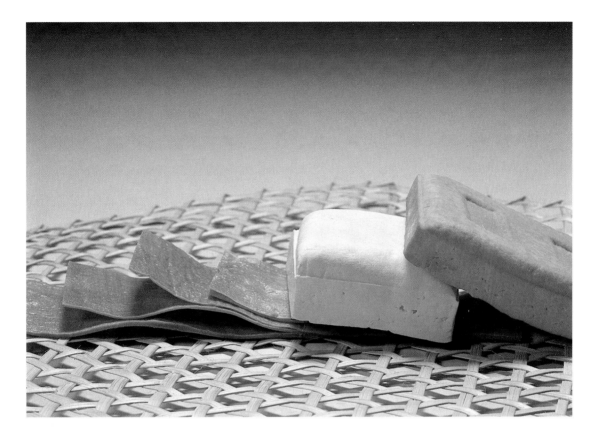

Season chicken or pork strips and prawns with **A** and leave aside.

Bring half a saucepan of water to a rapid boil. Scald noodles for under a minute. Drain with a large wiremesh skimmer and immediately plunge noodles into a basin of cold water for a few seconds. Drain well again and place in a dish. Mix noodles with oil and leave aside.

Heat oil in a *kuali* and lightly brown shallots and garlic. Put in mushroom strips and stir fry for a minute. Add seasoned chicken or pork strips and prawns and stir fry briskly. Add carrot, Chinese cabbage and stir fry for 1-2 minutes, then add bean sprouts. Add noodles.

Combine **B** and add to noodles. Toss well with a pair of chopsticks until noodles are well-combined with sauce. Throw in spring onion and coriander leaves and serve hot granished with shallot crisps and chilli strips.

Soyabean products:
(from left to right) dried sweet beancurd sheets (*tim chook*) – wipe clean with a damp cloth, then deep fry in hot oil before cooking to prevent from breaking; soft beancurd (*taufu*) – available from the local market and supermarket, this can be stored covered with water in the refrigerator for 2-3 days, if the water is changed daily; hard beancurd (*taukwa*) – used for stuffing, garnishing and deep frying.

Pork Chop Noodles

These are two unusual recipes. I prefer the dry version in which a combination of sauces flavours the noodles. For the soup, the flavour is mainly in the stock. The Szechuan vegetable, *char choy*, adds a unique taste to this dish.

Szechuan preserved vegetable (char choy)
This is preserved Chinese radish pickled in salt and chillies. Sold in jars in Chinese provision stores and supermarkets, the olive green vegetable is usually coated with chilli powder. Remember to wash well and soak in water for at least 30 minutes before using to reduce saltiness.

Preparation: 15 minutes
Cooking: 20 minutes (dry)/30 minutes (soup)
Serves: 4 persons

4 t-bone pork chops (1¼ cm), washed

A
½ teaspoon pepper
½ teaspoon salt
2 teaspoons sugar
¼ teaspoon bicarbonate of soda
1 tablespoon Chinese rice wine (p 55)
1 dessertspoon black vinegar
1 teaspoon chilli oil (p 33)
2 cloves garlic, ground
1 egg white, beaten

4 tablespoons oil

Trim pork chops. Using blunt edge of cleaver, lightly score the meat on both sides to tenderise. Marinate with **A**, adding the egg white last after all the other seasonings are well-blended with meat, for at least an hour.

Heat *kuali* with oil until hot. Reduce heat and deep fry pork chops for approximately 6-7 minutes until cooked through. Remove and leave aside.

Dry Pork Chop Noodles

300 g dried Chinese noodle sticks

A

½ tablespoon light soya sauce

1 teaspoon dark soya sauce

1 tablespoon Chinese rice wine (p 55)

½ tablespoon black vinegar

1 tablespoon chilli sauce

1 teaspoon sesame oil

½ teaspoon pepper

2 teaspoons sugar

1 teaspoon cornflour

¾ cup fresh pork or chicken stock (p 24)

3 tablespoons oil

2 cloves garlic, minced

1 tablespoon hot bean paste

90 g Szechuan preserved vegetable (char choy), *washed, cut into strips and soaked in water*

Boil dried noodles. Drain and mix with 2 tablespoons cooked oil (using remaining oil from frying pork chops).

Combine **A** with stock.

Heat oil in *kuali,* add minced garlic and hot bean paste and fry till fragrant. Add Szechuan preserved vegetable and stir fry for one minute. Add seasoned stock and simmer until sauce thickens.

Divide cooked noodles into 4 individual bowls. Add 2-3 tablespoons of the sauce into each bowl and mix well. Sprinkle in spring onion and top with pork chop. Serve hot.

Hot bean paste/sauce
Also known as chilli bean sauce or hot soyabean sauce, this is a mixture of fermented soyabeans and chillies. It's sold in jars in Chinese provision stores and supermarkets. Once opened, store in the refrigerator, keeping the cap and neck of the jar clean.

If it's not available, substitute it with soyabean paste mixed with 1 teaspoon ground dried chillies (*cili giling*).

Besides giving the world some of its best teas, the Chinese were also the first to enjoy tea in the garden. More than a thousand years ago, the cultured mandarins of Soochow and Hangchow sipped tea from fine porcelain cups in tea houses set among lotus-filled ponds and rustic bridges. The Japanese elevated such tea-taking into an art.

Pork Chop Noodles in Soup

300 g dried Chinese noodle sticks

1 piece Szechuan preserved vegetable (char choy, p 28), washed, cut into strips and soaked in water

5 cups fresh chicken stock (p 24)

A

1 teaspoon salt

¹/₂ teaspoon pepper

1 teaspoon dark soya sauce

¹/₂ teaspoon sesame oil

2 stalks spring onion, chopped

Drop noodles into a large saucepan of boiling water and cook for 8 minutes until noodles are just tender. Drain and divide into 4 serving bowls. Bring chicken stock to a boil, add Szechuan preserved vegetable and **A**. Simmer for 3 minutes and pour enough soup into each bowl to cover noodles. Sprinkle with spring onion and top with pork chop. Serve hot.

Hot Sour Noodles

Preparation: 15 minutes
Cooking: 20 minutes
Serves: 2 persons

120 g minced pork

A
½ teaspoon pepper
¼ teaspoon salt
½ teaspoon light soya sauce
300 g dried Chinese egg noodle sticks
2 tablespoons oil

30 g dried prawns, washed and chopped
120 g Szechuan preserved vegetable (char choy, p 28), washed and diced

B
6 cups chicken stock (p 24)
2 teaspoons sugar
½ teaspoon salt
1 tablespoon dark soya sauce
3 tablespoons light soya sauce
1 tablespoon black vinegar
2 tablespoons chilli sauce
2 tablespoons sesame paste
1 tablespoon sesame oil
1 tablespoon chilli oil (p 33)

30 g peanuts, roasted and chopped
30 g white sesame seeds, roasted
1 stalk spring onions, chopped

Season minced pork with **A**.

Bring a saucepan of water to a boil and add a little oil. Boil noodles for 8 minutes or until cooked through. Strain and place in individual serving bowls.

Heat 2 tablespoons oil in a large saucepan and fry dried prawns until fragrant. Add Szechuan preserved vegetable and minced pork. Stir fry for 1 minute. Add **B** and bring soup to a boil.

Add enough soup into each bowl of noodles. Sprinkle with a little chopped peanuts, sesame seeds and spring onions. Serve hot.

**Sesame seeds/
sesame paste**
These are small, flat, oval seeds that are available hulled and polished (white) and unhulled (black). In Chinese cooking, white sesame seeds are used mainly as a garnish and in making sweets and in fillings. Its 'nutty' aroma is more pronounced when roasted. The black seeds are used to make a thick sweet soup and as a garnish for sweets.

Sesame paste is obtained from grinding white sesame seeds. It's sold in cans or jars with the better quality paste having a layer of oil on the surface. This should be stirred well before using. If it's not available, substitute with creamy peanut butter.

Cha Cheong Meen
(Hot Spicy Noodles)

Another Szechaun noodle dish.

Preparation: 20 minutes
Cooking: 30 minutes
Serves: 4 persons

250 g pork with a little fat, finely diced

A
½ tablespoon light soya sauce
1 teaspoon Chinese rice wine (p 55)
1 teaspoon dark soya sauce
½ tablespoon chilli oil (p 33)
½ teaspoon sugar
½ teaspoon pepper
1 teaspoon cornflour

5 tablespoons oil
1 piece beancurd (taukwa, p 27), diced
1 large onion, diced
1½ tablespoon sweet bean paste (tim tau cheong)
3 cloves garlic, smashed and minced

**Sweet bean paste
(*tim tau cheong*)**
This is made from fermented soya beans, flour, sugar and spices. It's sold in cans and jars in Chinese provision stores or supermarkets.

B

2 tablespoons light soya sauce
1 teaspoon Chinese rice wine (p 55)
1 teaspoon dark soya sauce
1 teaspoon chilli oil
½ tablespoon sugar
½ teaspoon pepper
2 tablespoons water or fresh chicken stock (p 24) and 1 teaspoon cornflour, blended
1 tablespoon oil
600 g dried Chinese noodle sticks
1 small carrot, shredded
1 small cucumber, seeds discarded and shredded
2 cabbage leaves, shredded

Marinate pork with **A** for 30 minutes.

Heat 3 tablespoons of the oil and fry beancurd for 2 minutes. Drain. Add seasoned pork and saute for 5 minutes. Dish out and leave aside.

Add 1 tablespoon of the oil and fry onion until transparent. Drain. Add another tablespoon of the oil and stir fry sweet bean paste and garlic until fragrant. Add onion, pork, beancurd and **B**. When it comes to a boil, thicken with cornflour mixture. Dish out.

Bring a large saucepan of water to the boil. Add 1 tablespoon of oil to boiling water and put in noodles. Cook until soft and drain well.

Place noodles into 4 individual serving bowls. Arrange shredded carrot, cucumber and cabbage around the sides of the bowl. Top with 3-4 tablespoons of pork mixture. Serve immediately.

Chilli Oil

This is used extensively in Szechuan cooking. You can buy it bottled from Chinese provision stores and supermarkets or you can try making your own. Store the residue and use it for curries or for making your own chilli sauce (below). Surprise friends and family with your culinary skills!

15-20 dried chillies
8 tablespoons oil

Soak dried chillies in hot water till soft. Remove stems. (If a less pungent oil is preferred, cut the dried chillies into 2 and remove some of the seeds.) Place the soaked chillies in a blender with cooking oil. Blend mixture coarsely and pour into a saucepan. Cook over low heat for 3 minutes. Strain oil and keep in an air-tight jar.

Chilli Sauce

This can be used as a dip for meat, seafood and noodle dishes.

5 tablespoons cooking oil
1 tablespoon preserved soyabean paste
¼ teaspoon sugar
chilli residue from recipe above

Heat oil until hot and stir fry preserved soyabean paste over low heat until fragrant. Add sugar and add the chilli residue and mix well. Cool and store in an air-tight container.

Beef Shreds with Crispy Beehoon

Preparation: 20 minutes
Cooking: 15 minutes
Serves: 2 persons

100 g beef
A
¼ teaspoon bicarbonate of soda
¼ teaspoon salt
½ teaspoon sugar
½ teaspoon cornflour
2 teaspoons water
1 tablespoon oil
90 g carrot, shredded
60 g canned bamboo shoots, shredded
1 tablespoon oil
90 g beansprouts, heads and tails removed
oil for deep frying
90 g beehoon, *broken into approximately 5 cm pieces*
1 tablespoon oil
8 thin slices ginger, shredded
1 clove garlic, smashed and finely chopped
2 dried Chinese mushrooms, soaked and shredded
½ green pepper, cut into thin strips

B
⅓ teaspoon salt
⅓ teaspoon sugar
½ teaspoon sesame oil
1 teaspoon oyster sauce
½ teaspoon Chinese rice wine (p 55)
1 teaspoon dark soya sauce
½ cup water
¾ teaspoon cornflour

Slice beef thinly and smash each slice with the blunt edge of cleaver to tenderise meat. Shred beef and marinate with **A**, adding the oil last after all the other seasonings are well-blended with meat, for at least 30 minutes.

Put a little water to boil in a saucepan. Add a pinch of salt. Scald shredded carrot and bamboo shoots. Drain and leave aside. Heat *kuali* with oil and stir fry bean sprouts for 30 seconds. Remove and leave aside.

Wash *kuali* and reheat with 3-4 ladles of oil until hot. Turn off the heat. Add shredded beehoon. Stir fry quickly and drain well from the hot oil. Place on serving dish.

Discard excess oil except for 1 tablespoon in *kuali*. Lightly brown ginger and garlic. Stir fry mushrooms and shredded beef. Add scalded carrots, bamboo shoots and beansprouts. Add green pepper and pour in **B**. When mixture bubbles and thickens, pour mixture over beehoon and serve immediately.

Tea leaves come in a thousand different shapes, some look like the boots of a Tartar, some like the breast of a buffalo, some like clouds approaching from the mountains; some look like the rippling on the water caused by a breeze, some have a dull brown colour and look like freshly ploughed soil covered with puddles after heavy rainfall. All these are good teas.

(Lu Yu, *An Ode to Tea*)

Hong Kong Style Sar Hor Fun (Fresh Rice Noodles) With Beef

Preparation: 30 minutes
Cooking: 20 minutes
Serves: 2 persons

Ginger juice

Scrape the skin off a piece of thumb-size ginger, pound it into a pulp and squeeze this to obtain the required amount of juice. The pulp can be frozen and used in dishes such as curries requiring a little chopped ginger.

Fresh rice noodles

These are wide flat noodles produced by cutting thin sheets of steamed rice flour into strips. They're easily obtainable from the local market, supermarket or Chinese speciality stores and keep well for up to a week in the refrigerator and frozen for up to a month. Freeze in small amounts in plastic containers or strong plastic bags.

120 g beef, cut into thin slices

A

⅓ teaspoon bicarbonate of soda

1 dessertspoon ginger juice

½ teaspoon salt

¼ teaspoon sugar

2 teaspoons cornflour

1 tablespoon oil

5 small stalks mustard green (choy sum),
trim both ends with scissors

1 tablespoon oil

½ teaspoon salt

3 tablespoons oil

300 g fresh rice noodles, strands separated

1 tablespoon water or chicken stock and

1 tablespoon light soya sauce, combined

100 g beansprouts, tailed

36

B
½ cup + 1 tablespoon stock
½ teaspoon light soya sauce
2 teaspoons dark soya sauce
3 teaspoons cornflour

1 stalk spring onion and 1 sprig coriander leaves, cut into 2.5 cm lengths
2 tablespoons oil

Marinate beef with **A**, adding oil last after all the other seasonings are well-blended with meat, for at least 20 minutes.

Bring half a saucepan of water to a boil. Add oil and salt. Scald mustard greens until just cooked. Drain well and arrange on a oval dish. Turn off heat and scald beef. Allow to soak for 1 minute. Remove scum from the surface, then drain meat and leave aside.

Heat *kuali* with 1 tablespoon of oil. Ensure that the whole *kuali* is well-greased, then pour off excess oil. Put in rice noodles and toss in hot *kuali* for 2 minutes. Add combined stock with light soya sauce and stir fry till well-mixed. Remove and place on vegetables. Reheat *kuali* with another tablespoon of oil and stir fry beansprouts for 30 seconds. Remove and place over fried noodles.

Wash *kuali* and reheat with remaining tablespoon of oil. Add **B**, then meat, spring onion and coriander leaves. Lastly, stir in 2 extra tablespoons of oil.

Pour meat mixture over noodles. Serve with cut red chillies and light soya sauce.

Beef can be replaced with the following combination:

½ **a pig kidney**
½ **a pig heart**
10 slices of liver

Marinate as for beef.

Fried Beehoon With
Mixed Vegetables (1)

This is flavoured with oyster sauce and easier to prepare, not requiring frequent stir frying like the second recipe.

Preparation: 20 minutes
Cooking: 20 minutes
Serves: 6 persons

1 packet (600 g) beehoon, soaked in water until soft and drained
½ cup oil
6 shallots and 4 cloves garlic, minced
6 Chinese cabbage leaves and 1 carrot, cut into strips
300 g beansprouts, tailed

A
1 cup water
1 chicken cube
2 tablespoons oyster sauce
2 tablespoons light soya sauce
1 teaspoon sugar
½ teaspoon pepper
¼ teaspoon salt

3 eggs, made into thin omelette and shredded
1 small head lettuce, cut into strips
2 red chillies, cut into strips

Sambal Belacan

5 cm x 5 cm x ½ cm piece shrimp paste (*belacan*)
8 red chillies, seeded
3 local limes

Roast shrimp paste in a pan till fragrant. While hot, pound with red chillies till smooth. Put into a small dish and squeeze in lime juice.

Heat oil in *kuali* and fry minced onions and garlic until lightly brown. Add vegetables by piling one on top of the other in the following order – cabbage, carrots, beansprouts and lastly, *beehoon*.

Combine **A** and pour in. Do not stir. Cover *kuali* for 10 minutes. Remove cover and stir fry until well-mixed. Dish out on serving plate and garnish with omelette, lettuce and chilli strips. Serve with *sambal belacan*.

Fried Beehoon with Mixed Vegetables (2)

This Cantonese-style version is drier than the one before. Amounts given here are useful for parties but if you prefer to make a smaller quantity, just reduce all the ingredients by half.

Preparation: 20 minutes
Cooking: 25 minutes
Serves: 10 persons

1½ packets (900 g) beehoon, *soaked in water until soft and drained*
¾ cup oil
5 shallots, sliced
10 cloves garlic, minced
2 carrots, cut into strips
1 small cabbage, shredded
300 g beansprouts, tailed

A
¾ cup fresh chicken stock (p 24)
1 chicken cube
2 tablespoons light soya sauce
1 teaspoon pepper
½ teaspoon salt

5 eggs, made into thin omelette and shredded
2 red chillies, cut into strips
chopped spring onions and coriander leaves

Heat 1 tablespoon of the oil in a *kuali* and lightly brown half of the shallots and garlic. Add salt and carrots. Stir fry, adding a little water and cover *kuali* for 2 minutes. Remove cover, add cabbage and fry well. Dish out and leave aside.

Heat remaining oil in *kuali* and lightly brown remaining onion and garlic. Add beansprouts and *beehoon* without stirring. Combine **A** and pour in. Cover *kuali* for 5 minutes. Uncover and add fried vegetables. Mix well and dish out.

Garnish with omelette and chilli strips, chopped spring onions and coriander leaves. Serve hot or cold with chilli sauce.

Chinese Onion Pancakes

Preparation: 20 minutes
Cooking: 15 minutes
Makes: 6

180 g plain flour
³/₈ cup boiling water
½ egg, lightly beaten

½ tablespoon sesame oil and 1 tablespoon cornoil, combined
salt to taste

A
1 stalk spring onion, chopped
1 stalk coriander leaves (p 43), chopped
1 red chilli, chopped

4 tablespoons oil

Sift flour into a bowl and add boiling water. Mix with a wooden spoon. Add beaten egg and mix again until smooth. Leave aside for 20 minutes.

Knead on a lightly oiled surface until smooth and elastic. Roll into a long sausage roll and cut into 6 pieces. Using a rolling pin, roll each piece of dough into a flat 20 cm pancake. Brush surface lightly with combined oils. Sprinkle with a little salt and combined **A**. Fold two sides to the centre to slightly overlap. Lightly flatten with a rolling pin and roll up like a swiss roll. Roll out again into a round flat pancake.

Heat a shallow saucepan oil and fry pancakes on both sides until golden. Serve with chilli sauce.

Chilli Sauce

Makes approximately 1½ cups

12 large red chillies, seeded
3 cloves garlic
1 cup water

A
2 tablespoons tomato sauce
½ tablespoon vinegar
½ tablespoon sugar
¼ teaspoon salt
1 tablespoon oil

Put chillies, garlic and water in a blender and blend until fine. Pour into a small saucepan and add **A**. Bring to a boil. Reduce heat and simmer for 5 minutes. When cool, store in a glass jar at room temperature.

Leek and Chives Turnovers

Served as a snack or for breakfast.

Preparation: 30 minutes
Cooking: 15 minutes
Makes: approximately 12 rolls

1 tablespoon oil
4 dried Chinese mushrooms, soaked and cut into thin strips
300 g leek, finely sliced
60 g chives, chopped
120 g char siew (p 58) or chicken, finely diced

A
1 teaspoon salt
½ teaspoon pepper
1 teaspoon sesame oil

1 teaspoon cornflour
3 springs coriander leaves (p 43), chopped

250 g plain flour, sifted
¼ teaspoon salt
½ cup boiling water
¼ cup cold water

½ cup oil

Heat oil and fry mushrooms. Add leek, chives and *char siew*. Stir fry and add **A**. Cool and mix in cornflour and coriander leaves.

Put flour and salt in a bowl. Add boiling water and mix well. Add the cold water and mix again. Knead dough until smooth and elastic. Roll into a sausage roll and cut into 12 pieces.

Lightly flour the board and roll each piece into a thin circle. Place 2 tablespoons of the filling in the centre. Fold into half and press and seal the edges together to enclose filling.

Heat a shallow frying pan with ½ cup of oil and fry the turnovers on both sides over low heat until lightly browned and crispy. Serve with chilli sauce.

Fried Bean Curd Rolls

Using the same filling, you can also make Fried Bean Curd Rolls.

Preparation: 20 minutes
Cooking: 15 minutes
Steaming: 5 minutes
Makes: approximately 12 rolls

2 bean curd sheets (*foo pei*)

Put filling on a sheet of bean curd and roll into a swiss roll. Seal edges with cornflour paste. Steam over rapidly boiling water for 5 minutes. Cut into 5 cm pieces and deep fry until golden. Serve with chilli sauce.

Bean curd sheets (*foo pei*)
These are yellowish translucent sheets that are used for wrapping meat and vegetarian fillings. Look for soft, flexible sheets as the brittle ones will break easily when wrapping.

Chinese Ladle Cake

This crunchy savoury cake is great for snacks.

Preparation: 15 minutes
Cooking: 15 minutes
Makes: 16

16 medium-sized prawns, washed
180 g self-raising flour
60 g rice flour
60 g plain flour
1¼ teaspoons salt
½ teaspoon pepper
1¼ cups water
1 stalk spring onion, chopped
3 green chillies, finely sliced
1 onion, finely sliced
oil for deep frying

Shell the prawns leaving the tails and heads intact and trim the eye section using a pair of scissors.

Sift self-raising, rice and plain flours into a mixing bowl. Add salt and pepper and mix into a soft batter with water. Stir in spring onion, green chillies and onion.

Heat oil for deep frying. Heat a ladle in hot oil for 1 minute. Remove hot ladle and put in 1½ tablespoons of batter mixture to fill ladle. Place a prawn in the centre and press lightly. Deep fry until cake turns light golden. Loosen cake from the ladle with a small knife. Let it cook further for a minute or until cake turns golden brown. Drain on absorbent paper. Serve with chilli sauce.

Nonya Meat Cakes

Preparation: 30 minutes
Cooking: 30 minutes
Makes: 22

2 tablespoons oil	
90 g pork or chicken, minced	

A

2 teaspoonfuls sugar
1½ teaspoonfuls coriander powder
½ teaspoon pepper
½ teaspoon salt

210 g prepared green bean paste (see filling for ang koo on p 15)
1 tablespoon shallot crisps

250 g glutinous rice flour
1 cup coconut milk, from ½ grated coconut
60 g gula melaka (palm sugar), chopped
3 pandan leaves, knotted
2 dessertspoons cornoil

22 rounds (7 cm) banana leaves, greased

Coriander leaves, seeds and powder
Used as a seasoning and garnishing, the leaves are also known as Chinese parsley. They can be stored in an airtight container in the refrigerator for about a week. Coriander seeds are the main ingredient in curry powder and is probably the most frequently used spice in local cooking. Coriander powder is used as a seasoning for many dishes, particularly in Indian, Malay and Peranakan cooking.

Heat oil and stir fry meat with **A** for 5 minutes. Add green bean paste and cook until mixture is well-combined. Remove from heat and stir in 1 tablespoonful of shallot crisps. Cool.

Sift glutinous rice flour into a mixing bowl. Put coconut milk, palm sugar and pandan leaves in a saucepan and bring to a boil stirring until palm sugar completely dissolves. Remove pandan leaves.

Pour boiling coconut mixture into the glutinous rice flour and mix with a wooden spoon. Add cornoil and knead into a smooth soft dough.

Divide dough into 22 portions and form into round balls. Flatten each ball slightly and fill with 1 teaspoonful of filling. Gather the edges and seal to enclose the filling. Press ball of dough into a small greased *ang koo* mould (p 15). Tap the meat cakes out lightly and place on greased banana leaves.

Place in a steamer and steam over rapidly boiling water for 3 minutes.

Nonya Kueh Mah Chee

Kueh Mah Chee is a glutinous rice ball cake coated with sesame seeds (*chee mah* in Cantonese). This is a Nonya version of the *kueh*.

Preparation: 30 minutes
Cooking: 20 minutes
Makes: 15

60 g peanuts, roasted and coarsely ground
120 g grated white coconut
75 g brown sugar
¼ teaspoon salt

360 g glutinous rice flour
1 cup water, approximate
2 tablespoons roasted mung/green bean flour for coating

Mung/green bean flour (*luk tow fun*)
Available in Chinese provision stores. Otherwise, wash 1-2 kg of skinned green beans and sun-dry for a day or two. Then pan-fry or oven roast until fragrant. Grind it on your own or send to the mill for grinding, that is if you can still find one! This will keep well for months in the refrigerator or freezer.

Put peanuts, coconut, brown sugar and salt in a *kuali* and stir fry over low heat for 10 minutes. Remove and cool.

Sift glutinous rice flour into a mixing bowl and add enough water to form a soft dough. Divide into 15 portions and roll into round balls. Flatten each ball of dough slightly and fill with 1 teaspoonful filling. Pinch the edges to seal filling. Roll into a round ball again and lightly flatten.

Bring a pot of water to a boil. Drop in the *kueh*. Remove with a slotted spoon as soon as they float to the surface. Allow to dry a little then coat with roasted green bean flour.

Cheng Poh Leong / Cheng Tng

Literally this means 'clear soup'. It's a great dessert which can be taken either hot or cold. All the ingredients, except the quail's eggs, are available from Chinese medicine shops.

Preparation: 15 minutes
Cooking: 1½ hours

30 g lotus seeds (leng chee)
120 g gingko nuts (pak kor)
14 cups water
30 g pak hup
30 g dried longans
60 g pearl barley
360 g rock sugar
10 quail's eggs, hardboiled and shelled

Soak lotus seed for 15 minutes. Split and remove green centres. Blanch, skin and split gingko nuts. Remove embryos.

Bring water to boil, add washed lotus seeds, gingko nuts, *pak hup* and dried longans. Allow to boil gently until ingredients soften. Add pearl barley and rock sugar. Simmer over low heat until barley softens. Cool and chill in the refrigerator. Add quail's eggs.

Serve in small individual bowls hot or topped with crushed ice.

Groundnut Creme

Preparation: 15 minutes
Cooking: 20 minutes

330 g groundnuts, shelled and roasted
1 tablespoon rice flour
4 cups water
150 g sugar

Roast groundnuts till evenly brown. Cool and remove skin. Put groundnuts, rice flour and water in an electric blender and blend till very fine. Place blended ingredients and sugar in a saucepan. Bring to a boil over medium heat, stirring continuously with a wooden spoon. Allow to simmer for 5 minutes, stirring all the time. Serve in small bowls, either hot or cold.

Tow Suan
(Mung Bean Porridge)

A favourite with the Teochews for breakfast and as a snack. It's sort of 'gluey' and the thickening agent used is either water chestnut flour, which is more expensive and sweeter, or sweet potato flour.

Preparation: 15 minutes
Steaming: 20 minutes
Cooking: 15 minutes

300 g mung/green beans without shells, washed and soaked overnight
420 g sugar
7 ½ cups water
4 pandan leaves, knotted
4 tablespoons water chestnut or sweet potato flour, blended with ½ cup water
6 you tiau (chinese crullers) cut into 2 ½ cm pieces (p 48)

Drain mung beans and place in container lined with a piece of muslin cloth. Steam over rapidly boiling water for 20 minutes.

Put sugar and water in a large saucepan and bring to the boil stirring frequently. Add pandan leaves. Thicken boiling mixture with water chestnut or sweet potato mixture, stirring continuously.

Lift steamed beans from container with the help of the muslin cloth (this prevents the softened beans from breaking into smaller pieces), and add to boiling starchy liquid. As soon as it boils again, remove from heat. Serve hot with *you tiau*.

You Tiau
(Crisp Chinese Crullers)

I like to eat this sprinkled with crushed soft peanut cake – unusual but delicious. But I'm yet to try it dunked in hot black coffee, the way most Chinese love theirs.

Preparation: 30 minutes
Cooking: 20 minutes
Makes: 35

2 teaspoons sugar
³/₄ cup warm water
45 g compressed yeast
180 g strong flour, sifted
600 g plain flour
2 teaspoons baking powder
A
1 tablespoon salt
¹/₄ teaspoon ammonia
¹/₄ teaspoon potassium nitrate (huan)
(both are used to make the cruellers light, crispy and crunchy)
4 cloves garlic, finely ground
3 tablespoons cornoil
1³/₄ cups warm water

Strong flour
This is milled mainly from 'hard' wheats – varieties with a high gluten content. It is sometimes sold as 'bread flour' or 'high gluten flour' in supermarkets or speciality baking shops.

Dissolve sugar in warm water and drop in yeast. Stand for 15 minutes until frothy. Sift flour into a bowl. Add frothy yeast liquid and mix well.

In a separate bowl, sift flour and baking powder together. Add A. Beat well in an electric mixer using dough hook. Add yeast dough mixture and beat again until mixture is well-combined. Leave to rise, covered, for 2 hours or until mixture doubles in bulk.

Turn half of the mixture onto a floured board and with floured hands form into a long roll. Roll out into a 1.25 cm thick x 7.5 cm wide rectangle. Using a knife, cut into 1.25 cm wide strips. Pick up a strip and dot the 2 ends and centre with a little water, then place another strip on top of it. Using a chopstick, dip in flour and press through the centre lightly to join the 2 strips securely. Repeat process with remaining strips.

Heat oil for deep frying. Pick up the joined strips of dough at the ends, stretch lightly to a 25 cm piece. Drop in hot oil, turning continuously until golden brown. Remove and drain on absorbent paper. Serve hot.

Ham Chin Peng

Preparation: 1½ hours
Cooking: 1½ hours
Makes: 36

1 teaspoon sugar
1 cup warm water
45 g compressed yeast
250 g strong flour (p 48), sifted

A
720 g plain flour,
1½ teaspoons baking powder and
½ teaspoon bicarbonate of soda, sifted together
90 g castor sugar
2½ teaspoons salt
pinch of ammonia
2 cloves garlic, finely ground
2¼ cups warm water

B
1 tablespoon oil
1 teaspoon alkaline water

2 teaspoons five spice powder
bean paste filling

Dissolve sugar in warm water. Drop in yeast and stand for 15 minutes until yeast turns frothy. Sift strong flour into a bowl. Add frothy yeast liquid and mix well. Leave aside.

Combine **B** and add to **A** in a separate bowl. Beat well in an electric mixer using dough hook. Add yeast dough mixture and beat again until mixture is well-combined. Leave to rise, covered, for 2 hours or until mixture doubles in bulk.

Bean Paste Filling

250 g red beans
2 pandan leaves
5 cups water
½ cup oil
300 g sugar
1 teaspoon vanilla essence

Wash red beans and pandan leaves and put in a pressure cooker with water. Cook for 40 minutes until beans are soft. (If you don't have a pressure cooker and are using a normal pot, use 8 cups of water and cook over low heat for 1½ hours until red beans are soft.)

Blend beans to a fine paste in a blender. If beans are too dry and not turning in the blender, add a little hot water.

Heat oil in a *kuali*. Pour in bean paste and sugar. Cook, stirring all the time till bean paste is thick. (A non-stick *kuali* is best for frying red bean paste as the mixture tends to splatter. Bean paste can be left in a covered non-stick *kuali*, stirring occasionally before adding sugar. When bean paste is quite thick, add sugar, stirring until thick.) Add vanilla essence. Transfer to a bowl and cool to room temperature. Use as required.

(cont'd on p 50)

Turn half of the dough mixture onto a heavily floured board and form into a long roll. Sift half of the five spice powder evenly over surface of roll, then cut into 18 even pieces. With floured hands, shape into rounds. Flatten each round lightly and put a teaspoonful of bean paste filling in the centre. Gather and pinch the edges to enclose filling completely. Form into a round ball. Place on floured board and flatten with a rolling pin.

Heat oil for deep frying until hot. Fry over low heat a few minutes at a time turning frequently until light golden brown. Drain well on absorbent paper. Repeat process with remaining dough.

Wok Peang (Chinese Pancake)

Preparation: 10 minutes
Cooking: 20 minutes
Frying: 20 minutes
Makes: 6-8 pancakes

3 eggs
1 cup water
90 g sugar
180 g plain flour and 90 g cornflour, sifted separately
pinch of salt
sweet bean paste (see recipe for ham chin peng *filling on p 49), formed into golf-size balls*

Break eggs into a bowl and lightly stir with a pair of chopsticks. Add water, sugar and plain flour and mix well. Lastly mix in cornflour.

Heat and lightly grease a non-stick *kuali* and pour in a ladleful of batter. Quickly swirl the *kuali* around to spread the batter into a thin round pancake. Cook over low heat until pancake is set. Remove with a ladle and place on a plate. Repeat procedure until all the batter is used up.

Put a piece of thin pancake on a working board. Place a ball of sweet bean paste in centre and spread out thinly over pancake. Fold pancake into square.

Heat a lightly greased *kuali* and fry pancakes on both sides till lightly browned. Cut in wedges and serve hot.

D im Sum, the traditional Chinese lunchtime or brunchtime feast, is enjoyed wherever the Chinese have taken it. In some places it is known as *yum cha* ('drink tea') which one does a lot of while popping these wonderful appetisers into the mouth. The majority of *dim sum* dishes are steamed and braised. They are famous for their smooth, soft and delicate textures making the 'little hearts' so tasty and delightful. They 'touch the heart' – a literal translation of the two Chinese characters (点心). *Dim sum* is served piping hot in small servings placed in bamboo baskets with a variety of dips.

Dim Sum: (Clockwise from left) *Tau Sar Pow* (p 67), Chicken *Pow* (p 66), Three-Coloured *Siew Mai* (p 61), Kow Chee (p 70) Steamed Pork Ribs (p 78), Glutinous Rice *Siew Mai* (p 58) with chilli sauce, Siew Mai (p 61), *Tarn Tarts* (p 80), *Siew Pow* (p 68), Fried Flaky Meat Puff (p 64) and Crispy Chicken Rolls (p 60).

Fried Meat Patties with Saltfish

Preparation: 15 minutes
Cooking: 20 minutes
Makes: 8

60 g saltfish, thinly sliced
500 g pork with a little fat, finely minced
4 water chestnuts, finely chopped
3 slices ginger, finely chopped
1 stalk spring onion, finely chopped
1 egg

A
$1/2$ teaspoon salt
$1/2$ teaspoon pepper
1 teaspoon Chinese rice wine (p 55)
1 teaspoon sesame oil
$1/2$ tablespoon water
2 teaspoons cornflour

Heat a little oil in a *kuali* and fry salted fish over low heat until lightly brown and crisp. Cool and crumble into small pieces.

Combine minced pork with chopped ingredients and stir in egg and **A**. Throw meat against a board or into a bowl to improve its texture. Stir in fried salted fish. Form into small flat patties. Coat with extra cornflour and deep fry over medium heat until light brown in colour.

Serve with chilli sauce, red vinegar dip or ginger vinegar dip.

Ginger Vinegar Dip

2 tablespoons white vinegar
1 teaspoon sugar
5 thin slices ginger, finely shredded

Heat vinegar gently and stir in sugar until dissolved. Pour over ginger and leave overnight before serving as a dip.

Steamed Chicken with Saltfish

Preparation: 10 minutes
Steaming: 12 minutes

2 chicken thighs or 4 chicken wings, cut into 2 cm pieces

A
1 teaspoon salt
1 teaspoon sugar
1 teaspoon sesame oil
2 teaspoons light soya sauce
1/2 teaspoon pepper
2 tablespoons water
1 tablespoon cornflour
1 tablespoon oil

2 1/2 cm ginger, cut into strips
7 1/2 cm piece saltfish (threadfin), sliced and prefried

1 stalk spring onion and 1 sprig coriander leaves, cut into 2 1/2 cm lengths

Put chicken in a heatproof dish and season with **A** and ginger strips for 1 hour.

Add saltfish and steam chicken over rapidly boiling water for 12 minutes. Serve garnished with spring onion and coriander leaves.

Wine in Chinese Cooking
The best wine to use is *Hua Tiau* or *Shao Hsing Hua Tiau* Wine for Chinese cooking. Sold in light brown-coloured bottles, this is the finest quality Chinese yellow rice wine available and is more expensive than ordinary wine. Only a small amount will enhance the flavour of many dishes. It can be substituted with any other rice wine or sherry.

Steamed Beef Balls (1)

The water chestnuts and mushrooms in this recipe produce beef balls with a softer and smoother texture.

Preparation: 15 minutes
Steaming: 10 minutes
Makes: 36 walnut-size beef balls

A
600 g beef, finely minced
60 g chicken or pork fat, finely minced
5 dried Chinese mushrooms, soaked and finely chopped
3 water chestnuts
2 red chillies, minced

B
1 tablespoon Chinese rice wine (p 55)
½ tablespoon sesame oil
1 teaspoon sugar
1 teaspoon salt
½ teaspoon pepper
1½ tablespoons cornflour
½ tablespoon cornoil
1 stalk spring onion and 2 stalks coriander leaves, chopped
36 rounds (4 cm) cabbage leaves

The cabbage rounds can be easily stamped out with a sharp biscuit cutter.

Mix **A** with **B**. Marinate in refrigerator for 30 minutes.

Squeeze into walnut-size balls using a spoon dipped in cold water to separate the meatballs. Place meatballs on rounds of cabbage leaves. Arrange in a bamboo basket and steam over rapidly boiling water for 10 minutes.

Steamed Beef Balls (2)

This recipe produces a solid beef ball which is more 'meaty' to the bite.

Preparation: 15 minutes
Steaming: 15 minutes
Makes: 15 walnut-size beef balls

A
360 g beef, finely minced
60 g chicken or pork fat, finely minced
1 clove garlic and 5 cm ginger, ground and squeezed to obtain juice
1 medium-sized onion, finely chopped

B
1 teaspoon salt
½ teaspoon sugar
½ teaspoon pepper
1 teaspoon sesame oil
½ teaspoon light soya sauce
2 tablespoons cornflour

1 small egg white, lightly beaten
spring onion, chopped
coriander leaves (p 43), chopped
chilli, chopped

Mix **A** with **B**. Add beaten egg white. Refrigerate for 1 hour. Form into walnut-size balls and place in a heatproof dish.

Steam over rapidly boiling water for 15 minutes. Remove cover, sprinkle in a little chopped spring onion, coriander leaves and chopped chilli. Steam for 1 minute more. Serve hot, placed in small dishes in a bamboo basket.

Take water from a running stream and boil it over a lively fire; that from the springs in the hills is best and river water the next, while well water is the worst. A lively fire is a clear and bright charcoal fire. When making an infusion, do not boil the water too hastily, as first it begins to sparkle like crabs' eyes, then somewhat like fishes' eyes, and lastly it boils up like pearls innumerable, springing and waving about.

(Su Tung Po, *Brewing Tea in the Examination Room*)

Char Siew (Roast Pork)

Char siew can be bought from the market but to make the dish truly your own, try this recipe. You can serve your home-made *char siew* cut into slices with rice or noodles.

Belly or streaky pork has an alternating layer of fat and lean meat. The lean meat is very tender and juicy – just excellent for slow cooking like braising and roasting. The slow cooking further tenderizes the meat and renders out the fat effectively. At the butcher's, look out for belly pork that has thick layers of lean meat. To make preparation easier, have the butcher remove the rind and cut the meat into 3³/₄ cm strips for *char siew*.

Preparation: 15 minutes
Grilling: 30 minutes
Turbo boiler setting: 175°C

600 g belly pork or pork with fat

A
2¹/₂ teaspoons salt
4 tablespoons sugar
1 tablespoon light soya sauce
¹/₂ tablespoon thick soya sauce
1 tablespoon malt (*mak ngar tong*) combined with 2¹/₂ tablespoons hot water until syrupy
¹/₂ tablespoon red colouring, optional

(cont'd on p 59)

Glutinous Rice Siew Mai

Preparation: 30 minutes
Steaming: 6 minutes
Makes: 35

360 g glutinous rice
1¹/₄ cups water
¹/₂ teaspoon salt
3 tablespoons oil
5 dried Chinese mushrooms, soaked and diced
30 g dried shrimps, washed and chopped
180 g char siew, *pork or chicken, diced*

A
1 tablespoon light soya sauce
¹/₂ tablespoon Chinese rice wine (p 55)
¹/₂ teaspoon sugar
¹/₂ teaspoon pepper

2 stalks spring onion, *1 sprig coriander leaves and 1 red chilli, chopped*

35 wantan *skins (p 21)*
1 egg, made into a thin omelette with a pinch of pepper and shredded
35 green peas or 1 red chilli, chopped for topping

Wash and soak glutinous rice for 30 minutes. Drain and cook in a rice cooker with 1¹/₄ cups water and salt.

Heat *kuali* and stir fry mushrooms and dried shrimps until fragrant. Add diced *char siew*, pork or chicken. Add **A** and rice. Stir until well-mixed. Add spring onion, coriander leaves and chillies.

Trim off the corners of *wantan* skin to make them round. Place 2 teaspoons of the filling in the centre and gather the edge of the wrapper around the filling. Squeeze tightly to compress the filling. (If the filling is not well-compressed, the *siew mai* will lose its shape when steamed. If that happens, allow to cool and then reshape.)

Place in greased bamboo baskets and top with little omelette strips and press a green pea or chopped chilli in the centre. Steam over rapidly boiling water for 6 minutes. Serve hot.

Steamed Prawn Wrapped in Wantan Skin

Preparation: 30 minutes
Steaming: 10 minutes
Makes: 50

300 g shelled prawns, coarsely minced
200 g pork with a little fat, finely minced

A
5 water chestnuts, chopped
1 tablespoon chopped spring onion
1 tablespoon chopped coriander leaves
½ tablespoon Chinese rice wine (p 55)
½ tablespoon sesame oil
1 tablespoon cornflour
1 teaspoon sugar
¾ teaspoon salt
½ teaspoon pepper

48-50 wantan *skins (p 21)*
24 medium-size prawns, shelled, deveined with tails left on

B
¼ teaspoon pepper
¼ teaspoon sugar
¼ teaspoon salt

1 egg white, beaten, for sealing

Remove rind and wash pork. Dry with a clean towel. Cut into 3¾ cm thick pieces lengthways. Marinate with **A** for 5 hours, preferably overnight in the refrigerator.

Place marinated meat in a preheated turbo broiler or closed grill. Pour half of the marinade over the meat and cook for 12-15 minutes. Turn meat over and pour remaining marinade over meat and cook for a further 12-15 minutes, or until cooked through.

Mix chopped prawns and pork and stir in **A**. Leave for 30 minutes. Season whole prawns with **B**.

Take a *wantan* skin and put a teaspoonful of filling in the centre. Place a prawn on top of the filling. Brush another piece of *wantan* skin with a little egg white and cover prawn with this, brushed side down. Wrap the two skins around the filling and prawn, with the tail sticking out.

Place on lightly greased bamboo baskets and steam over rapidly boiling water for 10 minutes.

Crispy Chicken Rolls

Different fillings can be used for these rolls which are great for cocktail parties or buffets. You can use the recipe for Steamed Beef Balls (p 56) or the filling for Steamed Prawn Wrapped with *Wantan* Skin (p 59).

Preparation: 45 minutes
Cooking: 15 minutes
Makes: 12

---

240 g chicken breast

A

1 teaspoon light soya sauce

1/3 teaspoon salt

1 teaspoon Chinese rice wine (p 55)

1/4 teaspoon pepper

1 tablespoon water

B

180 g pork with a little fat, minced

90 g shelled prawns, minced

1 tablespoon crabmeat, optional

2 water chestnuts, minced

2 shallots, minced

1 stalk spring onion, minced

1 red chilli, minced

C

1/4 teaspoon five spice powder

1/4 teaspoon salt

1 teaspoon light soya sauce

1/2 teaspoon sesame oil

1/4 teaspoon sugar

1/4 teaspoon pepper

1 teaspoon cornflour

1 egg, lightly beaten

plain flour

Slice chicken breast across surface into 12 thin slices. Marinate with **A** for 30 minutes. Marinate **B** with **C** for 30 minutes in the refrigerator. Spread out the chicken slices. Place a teaspoonful of filling in the centre of each slice and roll up. Dip chicken rolls in beaten egg and coat with flour. Deep fry until golden in colour. Place on a plate garnished with lettuce.

Siew Mai (Dumplings)

If crab roe is unavailable, reserve 1 tablespoon of the filling, stir in 2 drops of orange colouring and use this as the topping.

Preparation: 1½ hours
Steaming: 12 minutes
Makes: 40

A
240 g well-minced prawns
240 g minced fatty pork
120 g cooked crabmeat

B
1 teaspoon salt
½ teaspoon sesame oil
dash of pepper
1 egg white

C
2 dried Chinese mushrooms, soaked and minced
3 water chestnuts, minced
1 stalk spring onion, thinly sliced

150 g wantan skins
1 tablespoon cooked crab roe

Season **A** with **B**. Stir in cornflour and cornoil. Beat the mixture with a spoon. Add **C**. Refrigerate the mixture for 1 hour.

Cut wantan skins into 7½ cm rounds with a biscuit cutter. Put 2 teaspoons of the filling in the centre and gather the edge of the wrapper to the top, letting it pleat naturally.

Place dumplings in greased bamboo baskets and sprinkle tops with crab roe. Steam for 12 minutes.

Three-Coloured Siew Mai

A variation with added colour.

Preparation: 30 minutes
Steaming: 10 minutes
Makes: 50

A
250 g small prawns, shelled and minced
60 g pork with a little fat, minced
3 water chestnuts, minced

B
½ teaspoon salt
½ teaspoon sesame oil
½ teaspoon sugar
¼ teaspoon pepper

½ tablespoon cornflour
1 stalk spring onion, finely sliced
150 g wantan skins (p 21)
5 cm carrot, diced
1 red chilli, diced
1 tablespoon green peas

Mix **A** with **B**. Stir in cornflour and beat mixture with a spoon. Add spring onion and refrigerate mixture for 1 hour.

Stamp wantan skins into 7½ cm rounds with a biscuit cutter. Take a piece of wantan skin and shape to form 3 loops. Fill each loop with filling and top with a green pea, a carrot and a red chilli. Arrange on greased bamboo baskets. Steam for 10 minutes.

Fried Wantan

Preparation: 45 minutes
Cooking: 15 minutes
Makes: 60

120 g small to medium-size prawns

A
½ egg white
1 teaspoon light soya sauce
½ teaspoon sugar
pinch of salt
dash of pepper

1 stalk spring onion, finely sliced
1 sprig coriander leaves (p 43), chopped
150 g wantan *skins (p 21)*
1 egg white, beaten
oil for deep frying

Clean and wash prawns. Dry with a tea towel. Cut each prawn into 2 or 3 pieces and season for at least 30 minutes with **A**. Add spring onion and coriander leaves.

Put a few pieces of seasoned prawns in one corner of a *wantan* skin. Roll up halfway and seal the two rolled ends with a little beaten egg white.

Heat oil for deep frying in a *kuali* and deep fry *wantan* till golden. Serve hot with chilli sauce.

Yam Puffs

Preparation: 1 hour
Cooking: 15 minutes
Makes: 34

2 tablespoons oil
4 cloves garlic, chopped
2-3 dried Chinese mushrooms, soaked and diced
120 g prawns, diced
180 g chicken, cut into small cubes
30 g green peas

A
1 teaspoon sugar
½ teaspoon salt
1 teaspoon light soya sauce
1 teaspoon oyster sauce
4 tablespoons water
½ tablespoon cornflour

1 sprig coriander leaves (p 43), chopped
1 stalk spring onion, chopped
1¼ kg yam, peeled and cubed

B
2 tablespoons sugar
3 tablespoons tapioca flour
pinch of five spice powder
2 tablespoons cornoil

oil for deep frying

Heat oil in a *kuali* and lightly brown garlic. Add mushrooms and stir fry. Put in prawns and chicken and fry for a minute. Add peas and combined **A**. Mix in coriander leaves and spring onion. Remove and cool.

Steam yam for 25-30 minutes until soft. While hot, mash until free from lumps. Add **B**. Knead well and shape into golf ball sizes. With lightly floured hands, flatten each ball into a round and put a teaspoonful of filling in the centre. Draw in and seal edge with a little water. Deep fry until golden brown.

Fried Flaky Meat Puffs

Two doughs are used to give the concentric layers for the circular pastry — quite attractive, and easy — to show off your culinary skills.

The chicken and potato filling can be substituted with curry puff filling (p 232) and to make shell curry puffs, use one piece of pastry, fill with filling and fold into half. Pinch and pleat the edges.

Preparation: 1 hour
Cooking: minutes
Makes: 20

250 g chicken, diced
A
1 teaspoon sugar
³/₄ teaspoon salt
¹/₄ teaspoon pepper
2 teaspoons light soya sauce
1 teaspoon sesame oil
¹/₂ teaspoon thick soya sauce
1 tablespoon oil
60 g carrot, diced
120 g potato, diced
1 tablespoon water
1 big onion
90 g green peas
1 teaspoon cornflour blended with 1 tablespoon water
1 stalk spring onion, chopped
1 sprig coriander leaves (p 43), chopped
Dough A
270 g plain flour sifted with 45 g self-raising flour
3¹/₂ tablespoons lard or vegetable shortening
¹/₄ teaspoon salt
³/₄ cup water
Dough B
90 g plain flour sifted with
90 g self raising-flour
3¹/₂ tablespoons lard or vegetable shortening

Marinate chicken with **A** for 15 minutes.

Heat $1/2$ tablespoon of the oil in a *kuali* and stir fry carrot and potato. Add water, cover the *kuali* and simmer till carrots and potato are soft. Remove and leave aside.

Heat *kuali* with remaining oil and fry onion until transparent. Put in chicken and stir fry until cooked. Add carrot and potato and lastly, peas. Stir in cornflour thickening and sprinkle in spring onion and coriander leaves. Cool before filling.

Sift plain and self-raising flours for **Dough A** into a bowl. Add lard or vegetable shortening, salt and water. Mix together to form a soft dough. Knead until smooth and leave covered for 30 minutes. Roll into a long sausage roll and cut into 20 pieces.

Mix ingredients for **Dough B** together. Form into a sausage roll and divide into 20 pieces.

Roll and flatten each piece of **Dough A** into a circle and place a portion of **Dough B** in the centre. Gather edges to enclose **Dough B**. Flatten again and roll out on lightly floured board, into a small rectangle shape. Roll up like a swiss roll. Repeat this procedure again ensuring the rectangle shape pastry is just a thin sheet.

Cut each roll into equal halves.Place cut side up and roll into a $7^{1}/_{2}$ cm flat circle. Put two teaspoonfuls of filling in the centre of uncut side. Place the other half of dough cut side out on top of the filling. Pinch the edges together and pleat decoratively.

Heat oil for deep frying and fry over medium-low heat for 5-6 minutes or until golden in colour.

Chicken Pow

Preparation: 1 hour
Cooking: 15 minutes
Steaming: 12 minutes
Makes: 35

---

720 g chicken, cut into small cubes

A

3 teaspoons light soya sauce

2 teaspoons thick soya sauce

3 teaspoons sesame oil

1½ teaspoons salt

1½ teaspoons pepper

---

5 tablespoons oil

4-5 onions diced

500 g turnip (bangkwang), diced

2 teaspoons cornflour blended with 2 tablespoons water

2 sprigs coriander leaves (p 43), chopped

Dough A

75 g compressed yeast

1 cup warm water

600 g plain flour

1 teaspoon salt

Dough B

360 g Hongkong flour

2 teaspoons double action baking powder

⅓ teaspoon bicarbonate of soda

150 g castor sugar

1½ tablespoons cornoil

½ cup water

Hongkong flour is a special wheat flour for *pows*. You can substitute with plain flour but it will require longer kneading.

Season meat with **A** and leave for 30 minutes.

Heat oil in *kuali* and lightly brown onions. Add chicken and stir fry. Add turnip and fry well. Thicken with cornflour thickening. Stir in coriander leaves. Dish out and cool.

Drop yeast in warm water and allow to stand for 10-15 minutes until yeast turns frothy.

Sift flour for **Dough A** into a deep bowl, add salt and make a well in the centre. Pour in the frothy yeast liquid and mix to form a firm stiff dough. Place dough on a lightly floured board and knead well for 10-15 minutes until smooth. Return dough to bowl and cover with a damp cloth. Leave to rise for 30 minutes or until doubled in bulk.

Sift ingredients for **Dough B** onto a clean board. Add castor sugar and mix well. Make a well in the centre and add cornoil and water. Gradually work in flour with fingers to form a soft dough.

Combine risen **Dough A** with **Dough B** and knead well for 10 minutes. When dough is smooth, form into a long roll and cut into 35 even portions. Shape into rounds.

On a lightly floured board, flatten each round with a roller and fill with chicken filling. Gather the edges of the dough around the filling by pleating the edges. Pinch and twist the pleats to enclose the filling (see diagram on p 69).

Place *pow*s on small rounds of greaseproof paper and arrange well apart in bamboo baskets. Place baskets in the steamer and steam over rapidly boiling water for 12 minutes.

Bean Paste Filling for *Tau Sar Pow*

The chicken filling can be substitued with bean paste filling.

500 g red beans
4 pandan leaves, knotted
8 cups water
1¼ cups oil
600 g sugar

Wash red beans and pandan leaves and put in a pressure cooker with water. Cook for 40 minutes until beans are soft. (Cook for 1½ hours, or until beans are soft, in a normal pot over low heat if you don't have a pressure cooker.) Place beans in a blender and blend into a fine paste.

Heat oil in *kuali*. Pour in bean paste and sugar. Cook, stirring all the time till bean paste is quite dry and sticky. Transfer to a bowl and cool to room temperature.

Siew Pow (Baked Dumplings)

The *siew pow* will have a lovely fragrance if lard is used. Chop the pork fat into small cubes. Fry over medium heat until the lard is slightly brown. Cool and store in the refrigerator. If done properly, the frozen lard should be white. If over-browned, it will be yellow and murky.

Preparation: 30 minutes
Cooking: 15 minutes
Baking: 30 minutes
Oven setting: 190 °C
Makes: 26-28

800 g chicken or pork, diced
A
2 teaspoons light soya sauce
3 teaspoons thick soya sauce
2 teaspoons sesame oil
2 teaspoons salt
1 teaspoon pepper
4 tablespoons oil
2 large onions, diced
4 teaspoons cornflour blended with ¼ cup water
2 sprigs corinader leaves (p 43), chopped
1 stalk spring onion, chopped
Dough A
180 g plain flour
105 g lard, melted
Dough B
240 g plain flour
60 g self-raising flour
2 tablespoons castor sugar
60 g lard
²/₃ cup water, approximate
1 egg white, beaten
1 egg yolk and 1 teaspoon evaporated milk , beaten to glaze

Season meat with **A** and leave for at least 30 minutes.

Heat oil in *kuali* and lightly brown onions. Add meat and stir fry over medium heat for 5 minutes. Add cornflour thickening and stir in chopped coriander leaves and spring onions. Dish out and cool.

Sift flour for **Dough A** into a bowl. Blend in lard and mix to form a soft dough. Roll out in between polythene sheets into a rectangle 20 cm x 30 cm and place in refrigerator.

Sift plain flour for **Dough B** with self-raising flour into a bowl. Stir in castor sugar and blend in lard. Add water and knead into a firm dough. Roll out on lightly floured board into a rectangle twice as long as **Dough A** but of the same width.

Remove plastic sheets from **Dough A** and place in the centre of **Dough B**. Fold over the two ends to cover Dough A completely. Seal edges and roll out pastry into a rectangle twice as long as it is wide and fold into three. Repeat rolling and folding procedure twice.

Divide pastry into two for easier handling and roll out one half thinly. Cover the other half with a tea towel to prevent drying. Stamp into 11½ cm rounds. Moisten edges with beaten egg white. Put two teaspoons of filling in the centre and gather the edges of the dough around the filling by pleating the edges. Bring pleats up to the top and lightly pinch to seal pleats.

Place on small rounds of greaseproof paper and arrange on baking trays. Bake in hot oven for 30 minutes until light golden in colour. Brush with egg glaze as soon as the dumplings are removed from the oven.

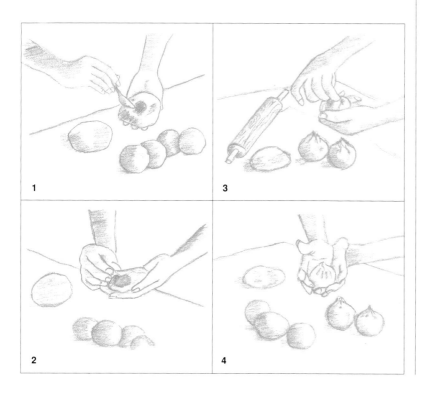

Kow Chee (Prawn Dumplings)

This dumpling has a special kind of pastry, *tang meen fan*, which is soft and silky smooth in texture.

Preparation: 1 hour
Cooking: 15 minutes
Steaming: 5 minutes each tray
Makes: 40-45 dumplings

4 tablespoons oil
2 shallots, minced
6 cloves garlic, minced
500 g small prawns, shelled and coaresly chopped
1 small carrot, shredded
300 g turnip (bangkwang), shredded and lightly squeezed to remove water
1 teaspoonful salt
¼ teaspoon pepper
2 sprigs coriander leaves (p 43), chopped
2 stalks spring onion, chopped
300 g plain flour
½ tablespoon salt
¾ cup water
3 extra cups water
45 g tapioca flour

Heat oil in *kuali* and brown shallots and garlic. Put in prawns and fry for 1-2 minutes. Add carrot and turnip and fry well. Add salt and pepper and lastly chopped coriander leaves and spring onions. Leave aside.

Sift flour into a large bowl. Add salt and ¾ cup of water. Mix until mixture forms a stiff dough and leaves sides of bowl. If necessary, add a little more water. Cover and leave to rest for 4 hours.

Add a cup of the extra water to the rested dough and carefully knead until liquid becomes milky white. Strain this flour liquid into a separate container. Add another cup of the water and repeat procedure with remaining flour. This process takes 10 minutes and as you knead the dough will become elastic and spongy in texture. (This spongy dough, gluten (*meen kan*), is used as a substitute for meat in many Chinese vegetarian dishes.)

Leave the bowl of milky flour liquid undisturbed for at least 6 hours or preferably overnight until flour settles to the bottom. Carefully drain or scoop off the clear yellow liquid from the surface and discard this. There should be approximately 2 cups of thick flour liquid.

Pour thick flour liquid into a non-stick *kuali* or saucepan and cook over moderate heat, stirring continuously to prevent mixture from sticking, for approximately 4 minutes until mixture turns into a transparent lump of dough. Remove from *kuali*.

Sift tapoica flour onto a board and turn hot dough onto tapioca flour and knead quickly until well-combined. Divide into 2 portions. Lightly flour board and roll out each portion to 3 mm thickness. Stamp into 7½ cm rounds. Put a dessertspoon of fillling in the centre and pleat edges using index finger and thumb leaving ¼ portion unpleated. Join the pleated and unpleated edges and pinch to seal.

Place dumplings in a steamer lined with banana leaves or well-oiled bamboo baskets. This prevents the pastry from sticking to the steamer and also gives a nice fragrance. Steam over rapidly boiling water for 5 minutes. Do not oversteam or dumplings will soften and loose shape. Serve hot or cold with chilli sauce.

Steamed Meat Dumplings

Preparation: 15 minutes
Steaming: 12 minutes
Makes: 32

A
360 g pork with a little fat, finely minced
120 g cabbage, finely chopped
30 g carrot, finely chopped
1 stalk spring onion, finely chopped

B
1 teaspoon sugar
1 teaspoon salt
1 teaspoon light soya sauce
1 teaspoon Chinese rice wine (p 55)
⅓ cup water
1 teaspoon sesame oil
1 tablespoon cooked oil (cooking oil heated and cooled)

240 g plain flour
pinch of salt
¾ cup boiling water

Mix **A** with **B** in a bowl. Lift mixture with the hand and throw forecefully into the bowl continuously for a minute to make the meat paste firm and smooth. Chill in refrigerator for 30 minutes before using.

Sift flour into a bowl and add salt. Pour boiling water onto the flour and mix quickly into a thick dough. Cover with a piece of cloth and set aside for 30 minutes. Knead for 5 minutes until smooth and sticky.

Roll into a long roll and divide into 2 equal lengths. Cover one roll and cut the other into approximately 16 pieces. Form each into a ball and roll out to about 7 cm rounds. Place a spoonful of filling a little off the centre. Pleat and seal pastry into a crescent-shaped dumpling.

Place dumplings on greased bamboo baskets and steam over rapidly boiling water for 12 minutes.

Fried Meat Dumplings
Heat a flat pan with 2½ tablespoons oil. Fry steamed dumplings on both sides until light golden in colour.

72

Steamed Vegetable Dumplings

Preparation: 45 minutes
Cooking: 20 minutes
Steaming: 7 minutes
Makes: 30

2 tablespoons oil
3 shallots, minced
2 cloves garlic, minced
250 g small prawns, shelled and chopped
A
1 teaspoon salt
½ teaspoon sugar
½ teaspoon pepper
500 g turnip (bangkwang), skinned and shredded
1 small carrot, shredded
¼ cup water
2 stalks spring onion, chopped
2 sprigs coriander leaves (p 43), chopped
225 g plain flour
90 g tapioca flour
½ teaspoon salt
1½ cups boiling water
1 tablespoon lard or vegetable shortening

Heat oil in a *kuali* and lightly brown onion and garlic. Add prawns and stir fry for 1 minute. Add **A**, turnip and carrot and stir fry for 5 minutes. Pour in water and continue frying until liquid evaporates. Stir in chopped spring onion and coriander leaves. Cool before using.

Sift plain and tapioca flours into a mixing bowl and add salt. Add boiling water gradually stirring well with a wooden spoon. Add lard and knead to a smooth dough. Roll the dough into a long sausage and cut into 30 even pieces. Flatten each piece of dough with a rolling pin in between plastic sheets. Roll out to form a thin round piece approximately 7½ cm in diameter.

Put 2 teaspoonsful of filling in the centre and gather the edges to the centre leaving a pea-size hole in the centre, or simply fold into half and seal edges.

(cont'd on p 74)

Arrange on a steaming tray lined with a piece of banana leaf. Steam over rapidly boiling water for 7 minutes. Brush with a little oil while hot.

Steamed Radish Cake

Preparation: 30 minutes
Cooking: 25 minutes
Steaming: 45 minutes

250 g rice flour, sifted
2 ½ cups water
¼ teaspoon salt

A
600 g pared shredded radish
½ cup water
¾ teaspoon salt
1 tablespoon sugar
1 teaspoon ground black pepper

30 g dried prawns, roasted and chopped
4-5 shallots, sliced and fried crisp (do not overbrown)

Mix rice, water and salt to make a watery batter.

Put **A** in covered saucepan and cook over low heat for 10-15 minutes until radish becomes soft and liquid evaporates. Add dried prawns and shallot crisps and pour in rice flour batter. Stir with a wooden spoon and cook for 3 minutes until mixture becomes a thick paste. Remove from heat.

Pour into a greased 20 cm cake pan. Smooth the surface with a plastic spatula and steam over rapidly boiling water for 45 minutes. Cool throughly before cutting into slices. Serve with chilli sauce.

Fried Radish Cake
Sliced radish cake is tastier when fried. Fry in shallow oil on both sides until lightly browned and crisp. Serve with chilli sauce.

Fried Spring Rolls

Preparation: 1 hour
Cooking: 30 minutes
Makes: 45

240 g chicken or pork, cut into thin strips
240 g prawns, diced

A
½ teaspoon sugar
½ teaspoon salt
1 teaspoon light soya sauce
1 teaspoon cornflour

3 tablespoons oil
4 cloves garlic
4 dried Chinese mushrooms, soaked and diced
600 g turnip (bangkwang), shredded and squeezed to get rid of excess water
1 small carrot, shredded

B
1 teaspoon thick soya sauce
½ teaspoon five spice powder
2 teaspoons light soya sauce
1 teaspoon sugar
dash of pepper

2 teaspoons cornflour mixed with a little water, for thickening
1 stalk spring onion, chopped
1 sprig coriander leaves (p 43), chopped

1 packet (about 50) 12½ cm squares spring roll skins
1 egg white, beaten
oil for deep frying

Season meat and prawns with **A**. Leave aside.

Heat oil in *kuali* and lightly brown garlic. Add seasoned meat and prawns, stir fry and dish out.

Put in mushrooms and fry for 1 minute. Add turnip and carrot and fry well. Stir in meat and prawns. Add **B** and cornflour paste. Stir in spring onion and coriander leaves. Dish out and cool.

Put 1 tablespoonful of filling on each spring roll skin, fold in sides and gently roll up. Seal edges with beaten egg white. Deep fry in hot oil and serve with chilli sauce.

Steamed Prawn Dumplings

Tang meen fun is non-gluten flour. It is easily obtainalbe from Chinese provision stores (I could even find it in Holland where I lived for sometime). However, if you have the time, it is far cheaper to make your own. Just follow the recipe for *Kow Chee* (p 70).

Preparation: 1 hour
Steaming: 7 minutes
Makes: 30

A
600 g medium-size prawns, shelled and coarsely minced
75 g pork fat, boiled and finely diced
6 water chestnuts, cut into thin strips
1 tablespoon crab roe, optional

B
1 teaspoon salt
1 teaspoon sugar
½ teaspoon sesame oil
½ teaspoon pepper
½ egg white
1 tablespoon cornflour
1 tablespoon lard, to be added last

230 g tang meen fun *(dumpling flour)*
1 tablespoon tapioca flour
½ teaspoon salt
1½ cups boiling water
1 tablespoon lard or vegetable shortening

Combine **A** with **B**. Stir vigorously with a pair of chopsticks until frothy. Refrigerate mixture for at least 30 minutes until firm.

Sift *tang meen* and tapioca flours into a mixing bowl and add salt. Stir in boiling water and lard and knead into a smooth dough. Cut into 30 pieces.

Grease a cleaver and work top. Flatten each piece of dough with the flat side of cleaver into a thin circle. A greased rolling pin can also be used or roll between plastic sheets. Fill with a teaspoonful of prawn filling. Fold into half and pinch the edges together. Gather the outside edge to form pleats. (An easier method would be to fold the dumplings into 'half-moon' or crescent shapes and press the edges together.)

Steamed Prawn and Bamboo Shoot Dumplings

Just follow the same method for the dough.

A
600 g medium-size prawns, shelled and coarsely minced
120 g canned bamboo shoots, cut into thin strips
4 dried Chinese mushrooms, soaked and chopped
6 water chestnuts, cut into thin strips
3 sprigs coriander leaves (p 43), chopped

B
1 teaspoon salt
1 teaspoon sugar
1 teaspoon sesame oil
½ teaspoon pepper
2 teaspoons Chinese rice wine (p 55)
1 tablespoon cornflour
1 tablespoon lard, to be added last

Mix **A** with **B** and refrigerate mixture for 30 minutes, or until firm, before using. Proceed as for Steamed Prawn Dumplings.

Place in greased bamboo baskets and steam over rapidly boiling water for 7 minutes.

Loh Mai Kai (Steamed Chicken Glutinous Rice)

Preparation: 30 minutes
Cooking: 15 minutes
Steaming: 90 minutes
Makes: 12

1½ kg chicken
A
4 tablespoons oyster sauce
2 teaspoons Chinese rice wine (p 55)
1 teaspoon thick soya sauce
2 teaspoons light soya sauce
2 teaspoons ginger juice (p 36)
1 teaspoon sesame oil
1 teaspoon sugar
½ teaspoon pepper
1 heaped teaspoon cornflour
1 kg glutinous rice
8 tablespoons oil
60 g dried Chinese mushrooms, soaked and cut into strips
8 shallots, sliced
B
2 teaspoons salt
1 teaspoon thick soya sauce
1 heaped teaspoon five spice powder
4 cups water
2 red chillies, seeded and sliced
2 stalks spring onion, chopped
4 sprigs coriander leaves (p 43), cut into 2½ cm lengths

(cont'd on p 78)

Debone chicken and cut into $1\frac{1}{4}$ cm thick slices. Season with **A** for at least 1 hour.

Wash and drain glutinous rice and steam for 45 minutes.

Heat oil in a *kuali* and fry mushrooms for 1-2 minutes. Drain oil and leave aside. Lightly brown shallots and put in glutinous rice and **B** and fry for 1 minute. Add water, mix well and simmer gently, covered, for 5-10 minutes. Remove from heat.

Grease 12 medium rice balls and put in some fried mushrooms and seasoned chicken at the bottom of each bowl. Fill with glutinous rice and press with the back of a spoon to fill three-quarters of rice bowl. Steam over rapidly boiliing water for 45 minutes.

To serve, turn steamed glutinous rice onto a small dish. Garnish with chillies, spring onions and coriander leaves and serve hot with chilli sauce.

Steamed Pork Ribs

The simplest to make of the *dim sum* dishes but ah, so tasty.

Preparation: 15 minutes
Steaming: 30 minutes

600 g meaty pork ribs, cut into 5 cm pieces

A
2 teaspoons cornflour
1 teaspoon thick soya sauce
3 teaspoons light soya sauce
1 teaspoon sugar
3 teaspoons preserved soyabeans (taucheo), minced
2 teaspoons salted black beans
4 cloves garlic, chopped finely
2 shallots, chopped finely
1 red chilli, chopped finely

Marinate pork ribs with **A** for 1 hour. Steam over rapidly boiling water for 30 minutes. Serve in small sauce dishes placed in bamboo basket.

Preserved soyabeans/ soyabean paste (taucheo)
This is a dark brown, salty paste made from black or yellow beans. It's in jars either as whole beans or in a paste and will keep for several months without refrigeration. The paste is salty, so don't use too much salt when using this.

Salted black beans
These are lightly salted, fermented black soya beans. Used as a seasoning, it's sold in packets in dry form and will keep indefinitely in dry conditions. They can be omitted if not available.

Meat Ham Balls

Preparation: 20 minutes
Steaming: 12 minutes
Makes: 10

500 g pork with a little fat, minced
2 slices ham, finely diced
60 g carrots, finely diced
2 tablespoons soaked fatt choy, *finely chopped*
1 stalk spring onion, finely chopped
1 egg
½ teaspoon sugar
½ teaspoon salt
½ teaspoon pepper
½ teaspoon sesame oil
1 teaspoon light soya sauce
1 teaspoon Chinese rice wine (p 55)
1 tablespoon cornflour

Combine all the above ingredients and throw meat against a board or bowl continously for 1 minute. Form into golf-size balls and arrange on greased heatproof dish.

Steam over rapidly boiling water for 12 minutes. Serve with chilli sauce, red vinegar dip or ginger vinegar dip (p 54).

Fatt choy, literally means prosperity. It's also known as black moss and commonly referred to as the 'hair' vegetable. It's a type of dried seaweed and is a must in the preparation of festival dishes especially during the Chinese New Year.

Tarn Tarts (Egg Tarts)

A common dessert for *dim sum*.

Preparation: 1 hour
Baking: 35 minutes
Oven setting: 175 °C
Makes: 24

Dough A
300 g plain flour
3½ tablespoons lard or melted butter, cooled
¼ teaspoon salt
¾ cup water

Dough B
180 g plain flour
3½ tablespoons lard or melted butter, cooled

240 g sugar
1¼ cup hot water
2 tablespoons milk powder
¼ teaspoon salt
½ teaspoon vanilla essence
6 medium-sized eggs

Sift flour for **Dough A** into a mixing bowl. Make a well in the centre and add lard, salt and water. Mix and knead to form a soft smooth dough. Cover dough with a tea towel and leave to rest for 30 minutes.

Mix flour and lard for **Dough B** to form a soft dough. Divide into 24 equal portions.

Dissolve sugar in hot water and stir in milk powder and salt. Cool and add vanilla essence.

Break eggs into a separate bowl and lightly stir with a fork. Do not beat. Pour cooled milk mixture into eggs and mix well. Strain mixture into a jug with a beak for easy pouring.

Take rested **Dough A** and roll into a long suasage roll. Divide into 24 equal portions. Flatten each portion and place a round of **Dough B** in the centre. Wrap and seal the edges. Shape into a round ball.

Roll out each ball of pastry on a lightly floured board. Fold into 3 layers by drawing the two opposite edges to overlap in the centre. Fold the remaining edges the same way. Roll out each piece into a 9-10 cm circle, or roll out into a thin circle large enough to stamp out 9-10 cm circles with a pastry cutter. Line egg tart patty tins with pastry. If desired, pleat the edges decoratively. Carefully pour custard mixture into pastry-lined moulds.

Bake in moderate oven for 5 minutes. Cover and continue baking for a further 30-35 minutes until set.

The End of Ramadan

Muslims celebrate *Hari Raya Puasa* after a month-long fast in which they abstain from food and drink between sunrise and sunset. During this month of *Ramadan*, they reflect on their faith, praying regularly and being free from evil thoughts and deeds. Two weeks before the *Hari Raya*, families start cleaning their homes, preparing *kuih* and weaving the *ketupat* casings for the celebrations at the end of the *puasa* (fasting).

On the eve of *Hari Raya*, traditional foods are prepared deep into the night. *Rendang, serunding, ketupat* and *lemang* make up the feast for family and friends. But despite all the delicious food, new clothes and merry-making, there is also a serious view to the festivities. The traditional greeting is accompanied by seeking forgiveness for all wrong doing during the past year and alms must be given to the poor.

MALAY DELIGHTS

Hari Raya feast: (clockwise from top, left) Rich Indonesian Layer Cake (p 217), Jelly-Layered Gateau (p 212), (in tray) *Kuih Kapit* (p 137), Vanilla Swirls (p 224), Quick and Easy Pineapple Tarts (p 228), Chequered Biscuits (p 221) and (in centre) Featherlite Jam Cookise (p 223); *Rendang Masak Hitam Manis* (p 89), *Serunding Daging* (p 91), *Lemang* (p 89) and *Ketupat Bawang* (p 87).

Roti Jala (Lacy Pancakes)

The net-like or *jala* ('net' in Malay) effect is achieved by pouring the batter through a special cup that can be bought from Malay shops or even the local supermarket. A good substitute is a kitchen funnel – use your forefinger to slightly close off the opening and let the batter run through. Or you could make a few small holes in the base of a condensed milk tin and use that. I've also seen Malay women in the kampungs dipping their hands into the batter and letting it trail off their fingers for the right effect – you might want to try that!

Preparation: 30 minutes
Cooking: 30 minutes
Makes: 24

240 g plain flour
½ teaspoon salt
2 eggs, beaten
2½ cups coconut milk, from ½ grated white coconut

Sift flour into a bowl and add salt. Stir in beaten eggs and coconut milk and beat until smooth. Strain batter if it is lumpy.

Grease and heat a non-stick pan on low heat. Put a ladleful of batter into a *roti jala* cup with four funnels and move it in a circular motion over pan so that pancake will have a lacy pattern. Cook until set. Turn over onto a dish. Continue frying pancakes until batter is used up.

When cool, fold pancakes into two or fold and roll up. Serve with *Curry Kapitan* (p 86) or *Ayam Percik* (p 85).

Ayam Percik

Preparation: 30 minutes
Cooking: 1 hour

1 kg chicken, cut into bite-size pieces

A
100 g fresh red chillies
10 bird chillies (p 94)
2½ cm turmeric root (kunyit hidup)
3 cm ginger
200 g shallot
1 stalk lemon grass, sliced
1½ teaspoon salt

2 stalks lemon grass, bruised (for added fragrance)
4 cups coconut milk, from 2 grated coconuts
2 double lime leaves (daun limau purut), *finely sliced*
1 small piece young turmeric leaf, finely sliced

Grind **A**. Marinate chicken with half of **A** for ½ an hour.

Place other half of **A**, bruised lemon grass and coconut milk in a cooking pot. Cook over low heat for approximately 25 minutes. Add marinated chicken and cook until chicken is tender and gravy, thick and almost dry. Lastly, add double lime leaves and turmeric leaves.

Serve with *Roti Jala* (p 84), or rice and tomato and cucumber slices.

Curry Kapitan

Belacan (dried shrimp paste) is commonly used in Malay curries.

Preparation: 30 minutes
Cooking: 40 minutes

4 tablespoons oil
2 onions, diced
2 teaspoons salt
A
15 red chillies
2½ cm piece turmeric
4 cloves garlic
15 shallots
10 candlenuts
2½ x 5 cm piece dried shrimp paste (belacan)
4 pieces 7½ -10 cm length lemon grass, thinly sliced
1 cup thick coconut milk and 3 cups thin coconut milk,
from 1 grated coconut
1 ½ kg chicken, cut into bite-size pieces
juice of 2 local limes

Ground **A**. Heat oil in a *kuali* and lightly brown onions with salt. Add **A** and fry till fragrant, adding a little of the thick coconut milk to prevent ingredients from sticking to pan.

Add chicken and fry well. Add thin coconut milk and simmer till chicken is tender, then put in remaining thick coconut milk and, when curry boils, the lime juice.

Serve with *Roti Jala* (p 84) or plain rolls.

Ketupat Bawang

Diamond-shaped rice dumpling that is a must for *Hari Raya*.

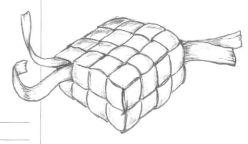

Preparation: 30 minutes
Cooking: 3$\frac{1}{2}$ hours
Makes: 25 *ketupats*

900 g rice
25 ketupat bawang *baskets*
enough water to cover ketupat

Wash rice and drain in a colander. Rice has to be quite dry and grainy to make filling easier.

Pull the tail end or the top of the *ketupat* casing open. Half fill each casing with rice. Pull the tail end to tighten. Boil in a large pot of water for 3$\frac{1}{2}$ to 4 hours.

Serve with *Rendang Masak Hitam Manis* (p 89).

Ketupat bawang casing is made from the young leaves of the coconut tree. The 'bone' of the leaf is removed making two halves which is then cleverly weaved like a mat into a basket. If you cannot find coconut leaves to make the casing buy readymade casings from the local market. If this is still difficult to obtain, make *Nasi Himpit* which is rice cake without the basket.

Nasi Himpit

Prepration: 30 minutes
Cooking: 30 minutes
Makes: approximately 60 cubes (allot 12 cubes per person)

600 g rice
4 $\frac{1}{2}$ cups water
pinch of salt

Wash rice, drain and put in a rice cooker. Add water and salt and cook till rice is done. Stir and mash with a wooden spoon while it is still hot. Transfer to a 25 x 15 cm rectangular dish or tin with a flat lid a little bit smaller than the dish or tin. Press lid firmly onto rice and place a heavy object on top to compress rice. Leave overnight in the refrigerator. Cut into 2$\frac{1}{2}$ cm cubes and leave aside.

Lemang (facing page)

Rendang Masak Hitam Manis

Preparation: 30 minutes
Cooking: 1 hour

500 g beef, cut into 1cm slices
A
15 dried chillies, soaked (p 94)
15-20 bird chillies (p 94)
15 shallots
2 cloves garlic
2 cm ginger
3 cm galingale (lengkuas)
2 stalks lemon grass, sliced
3 tablespoons oil
½ tablespoon thick soya sauce
2 tablespoons tomato sauce
3 cups coconut milk, from 1½ grated coconuts
1½ teaspoons salt
½ tablespoon sugar
3 stalks curry leaves

Grind **A**. Marinate beef with **A** for ½ an hour.

Heat 3 tablespoons oil in a cooking pot and fry beef mixture for 5 minutes. Add thick soya and tomato sauces, coconut milk and salt. Simmer until mixture becomes thick. Add sugar and curry leaves. Reduce heat, stir continuously until dry.

Serve with *Ketupat* (p 87) or rice.

Lemang (Bamboo Glutinous Rice Rolls)

This is a firm *Hari Raya* favourite and is usually prepared by the elders in the kampung where bamboo and firewood are readily available. It is so important with most kampung folk that wives would quarrel bitterly with their husbands if glutinous rice is not purchased for this speciality to celebrate *Hari Raya*.

(cont'd on p 90)

Lemang would taste best cooked in bamboo but an acceptable alternative is *ketupat pulut* (glutinous rice rolls wrapped in banana leaves and steamed). It will keep for 3-4 days without refrigeration if the glutinous rice is throughly washed until the water is clear.

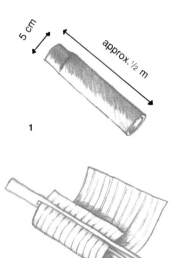

1

2

3

Preparation: 1 hour
Cooking: 4 hours

4 kg glutinous rice
4 tablespoons coarse salt
approximately 12 cups coconut milk, from 5 grated coconuts
24-26 green bamboos
24-26 young banana leaves, long edges trimmed, cut into pieces 5 cm longer than bamboos
firewood

Wash glutinous rice thoroughly and leave to soak for 1 hour. Drain and put rice in a large container. Add salt and enough coconut milk to cover rice completely. Mix well to dissolve salt.

Line each stick of bamboo with banana leaf (underside rolled in). This can be done easily with a banana leaf stem split through three-quarters down. Clip the long edge of the leaf in between the split banana stem, then roll up tightly. Thread into hollow bamboo. Carefully remove the banana stem, then stamp the bamboo on the ground to ensure that the banana leaf goes right down to the bottom.

Using a dessertspoon, fill four-fifths of the lined bamboo with rice and just enough coconut milk to cover the rice. Stamp the filled bamboo a couple of times on the ground to firmly pack the rice. Fold and tuck in the top end of banana leaf to seal rice. Start a fire. Place bamboos in a neat row against a steel pole two-thirds of a metre away from the fire and cook for 3^1/$_2$-4 hours, turning bamboos frequently to prevent burning. While turning the bamboos, stamp again a couple of times to pack rice firmly.

When rice is cooked, split the bamboos with a sharp knife. Cut glutinous rice rolls into 2^1/$_2$ cm thick pieces. Serve with *Rendang* (p 89) or *Serunding Daging* (p 91).

Serunding Daging

This is specially prepared for *Hari Raya* and wedding feasts. It's very time-consuming and entails a lot of work but the effort is worth the delicious dry curry in the end. It goes well with all rice dishes (*Ketupat, p* 87; *Nasi Himpit,* p 87; *Lemang,* p 88) and is also delicious on toast. Well prepared, it will keep for months in the refrigerator.

Preparation: 30 minutes
Cooking: 2 hours

300 g beef
A
15 dried chillies (p 94), soaked
10 shallots
2 cloves garlic
2 stalks lemon grass
*2½ cm galingale (*lengkuas*)*
1¼ cm ginger
*2½ cm square dried shrimp paste (*belacan*)*
2 tablespoons coriander powder (p 43)
1 teaspoon cummin
*2 double lime leaves (*daun limau purut*), sliced finely*
1 turmeric leaf, slice finely
1 heaped teaspoon tamarind paste mixed with
3 tablespoons water, strained
1 tablespoon sugar
1 cup coconut milk, from ½ grated coconut
½ white coconut, grated and dry-roasted till light brown
1½ teaspoons salt

Grind **A**.

Simmer beef in a saucepan for 1 hour with enough water to cover meat, or put in a pressure cooker and cook for 30 minutes. Remove and drain in a colander until dry and cool. Cut into 2½ cm cubes, then break meat with fingers into small pieces.

Marinate meat with **A**. Leave for 15 minutes.

Put marinated meat and coconut milk in a *kuali* and bring to a slow boil. Lower heat and fry continuously until almost dry, then add coconut and salt to taste. Cook for a further 30 minutes on very low heat, stirring all the time until completely dry.

Otak-Otak Udang dan Ikan

The favourite *otak* done the simple way without coconut leaves. The *kadok* leaves used give a strong distinctive flavour to the *otak-otak*.

Preparation: 30 minutes
Baking: 30 minutes
Oven setting: 175°C
Makes: approximately 30 pieces

250 g Spanish mackerel (ikan tenggiri), *cut into thin slices*
100 g shelled prawns, coarsely chopped
½ teaspoon salt
½ teaspoon pepper

A
1 stalk lemon grass, sliced
2½ cm turmeric root
50 g shallots
2 cloves garlic
2 slices galingale (lengkuas)
2 candlenuts
2 cm square piece dried shrimp paste (belacan), *toasted*

⅜ cup thick coconut milk, from 1 grated coconut
1½ tablespoons cornflour
1 teaspoon coriander powder (p 43)
½ teaspoon salt
2 large eggs
2 double lime leaves (daun limau purut), *finely sliced*

17 cm x 24 cm baking dish
tin foil to line baking dish
oil
3 kadok *leaves (optional)*

Kadok Leaves
This is a creeper that grows wild. It's sometimes chewed with betel nut and lime.

Grind **A**. Season fish and prawns with salt and pepper for 15 minutes.

Combine **A** with thick coconut milk, cornflour, coriander powder and salt. Put in seasoned fish and prawns. Add eggs and double lime leaves and mix well. Do not beat mixture.

Line baking dish with tin foil and grease with a little oil. Place 3 *kadok* leaves on the base of dish and carefully pour in fish mixture. Bake in a preheated moderately hot oven for 30-35 minutes or until light golden brown. Remove and place on a dish. Garnish with shelled steamed prawns, if desired. Serve with toast or rice.

Mee Goreng

The Chinese noodle with the spices of India and a true Malaysian dish.

Preparation: 30 minutes
Cooking: 20 minutes

1 potato
4 tablespoons oil
A
12 dried chillies (p 94), soaked
1 large onion
4 cloves garlic
1 large onion, sliced
150 g bean sprouts
300 g fresh yellow noodles
1 egg
B
150 g small/medium-sized prawns, shelled
2 tomatoes, quartered
1 teaspoon salt
2 tablespoons tomato sauce
3 green chillies, sliced
1 stalk spring onion, chopped
½ cucumber, sliced

Grind **A**. Boil potato for 10 minutes. Skin and cut into small cubes.

Heat 2 tablespoons oil in *kuali* and fry **A** over low heat for 5 minutes until fragrant. Dish out and leave aside. Heat remaining oil. Fry onion until transparent, then add bean sprouts and potato, and stir fry quickly for 1 minute. Put in noodles and fry well for 3-4 minutes.

Make a well in the centre, add egg, then **B** and stir well. Put in **A** and mix well. Just before removing from heat, add green chillies and spring onion. Serve garnished with sliced cucumber.

Chillies - an almost must with Asian cooking.

Fresh chillies (top) are ground for cooking or sliced thinly and served with soya sauce as a dip by the Chinese with many dishes especially noodles. Choose the hotter slender pointed ones for cooking, and the fat ones for garnishing. You may find it convenient to buy a large amount of fresh chillies and grind them in a blender or food processor with a little salt until you get a coarse paste. Pack 4-6 teaspoons (about 8-12 whole chillies) and store in the freezer. Allow to thaw before using, draining off any liquid before frying.

The smaller variety, *cili padi* or bird's eye chilli (left), is fiery hot. They are used either in their unripe green state or when they are red ripe. Flavour and heat intensify with ripeness, so be sure of what the recipe specifies.

Dried chillies (right) are used to lend spicy hotness and flavour. Choose the pointed more wrinkled variety which are more pungent and give a better flavour. Note that the flatter, neater variety is dried by a chemical agent. Tear each dried chilli into 3 or 4 pieces and soak in hot water for about 10 minutes. Sqeeze out excess water before grinding with a mortar and pestle or electric blender.

When buying chilli powder (centre), make sure it is fresh and fragrant. Remember to mix it with a little water before frying to prevent it from sticking to the pan. If it does stick before being well-fried, sprinkle in a little water.

Kuih Badak

Preparation: 30 minutes
Frying: 15 minutes
Makes: 22

A
240 g shelled fresh prawns, roughly chopped
6 tablespoons grated white coconut
12 shallots, thinly sliced
3 red chillies, seeded and finely sliced
3 green chillies, seeded and finely sliced
3½ cm fresh turmeric, ground
2 stalks (7½ cm length) lemon grass, ground
1 teaspoon salt
420 g plain flour
½ teaspoon salt
180 g margarine
1 egg yolk, beaten
¼ cup cold water, approximate
22 dried prawns, washed and drained

Combine **A** in a mixing bowl and leave aside.

Sift flour into a bowl and add salt. Rub in margarine with a pastry cutter until mixture resembles find breadcrumbs. Make a well in centre of flour mixture and add beaten egg yolk and water. Mix to a soft dough. It may be necessary to add a little extra cold water. Roll out pastry, half at a time to ¼ cm thickness and cut into 9 cm rounds.

Fill with 1 dessertspoon of the filling, gather up edges and seal at the top. Press a dried prawn where the pastry is sealed. Deep fry in hot oil until golden. Serve hot.

Rojak Suun

An unusual dish that uses the Chinese *tunghoon*, *suun* in Malay.

Preparation: 30 minutes
Cooking: 15 minutes

300 g transparent noodles (tunghoon/suun)
300 g bean sprouts
600 g potatoes
oil for deep frying
5 firm soyabean cakes
3 cucumbers, sliced
2 small bunches local lettuce

A
15 dried chillies (p 94), soaked
150 g dried prawns, washed, dried and toasted
1 tablespoon sesame seeds, toasted
3 cloves garlic

2 teaspoons salt
1 tablespoon vinegar
2 teaspoons sugar

Grind **A**.

Scald transparent noodles, then beansprouts in boiling water. Drain. Boil potatoes until cooked, then peel and cut into small cubes. Heat oil and deep fry soyabean cakes until light brown in colour. Cut into halves then slice.

Combine transparent noodles, beansprouts, potatoes, soyabean cakes and cucumbers in a bowl then place in a dish garnished with lettuce leaves.

Just before serving combine **A** with salt, vinegar and sugar. Mix well and pour over vegetables.

Rojak Tauhu

A very nutritious snack or meal.

Preparation: 15 minutes
Cooking: 20 minutes

A
35 bird chillies (p 94) and 2 teaspoons garlic flakes, ground

60 g palm sugar (gula melaka), chopped
8 small limes
1¼ cups water
1 tablespoon sugar
1 teaspoon salt

3 tablespoons oil
300 g raw shelled peanuts
oil for deep frying
5-6 firm soyabean cakes
240 g beansprouts, tailed and scalded
2 cucumbers, peeled and cut into small wedges

Combine **A** with palm sugar in a mixing bowl. Squeeze in lime juice through a strainer, mix well and add water, sugar and salt. Stir well and leave aside.

Heat 3 tablespoons oil in a *kuali* and fry peanuts until light golden in colour. Drain from oil, cool then rub to separate skin. Pound peanuts coarsely and leave aside.

Heat oil and deep-fry soyabean cakes until lightly browned on both sides. Drain, cool and cut into small cubes.

Combine scalded beansprouts, cucumber wedges and fried soyabean cubes in a dish. Just before serving, pour *rojak* sauce over vegetables.

Pecal

This is the typical Malay version of the *rojak* that is very propular in northern Malaysia, especially Perak. It has a wider variety of vegetables than the other *rojak* recipes in this collection.

Preparation: 30 minutes
Cooking: 20 minutes

300 g water convolvulus (young shoots only), cut into 5 cm lengths

300 g young tapioca leaves (tender shoots only), cut into 5 cm lengths

150 g bean sprouts, tailed

150 g turnip (bangkwang), shredded coarsely

150 g long beans cut into 5 cm lengths

1 medium carrot, shredded coarsely

1 cucumber, soft centre discarded, shredded coarsely

2 firm soyabean cakes, diced and fried

4 hardboiled eggs, quartered

1 tablespoon oil

2 tablespoons tamarind paste

1/2 cup water

1 tablespoon oil

A

15 dried chillies (p 94), soaked

2 1/2 cm square dried shrimp paste (belacan), toasted

1 1/4 cups water

B

4 tablespoons brown sugar

2 tablespoons black shrimp paste (heiko) and

1 tablespoon water, mixed

1/2 teaspoon salt

300 g roasted peanuts, ground coarsely

10 shallots, sliced and fried

3 cloves garlic, sliced and fried

Scald vegetables, except cucumber, separately in boiling water. Do not overcook. Drain well and arrange on a dish together with cucumber, fried soyabean cakes and hardboiled eggs.

Heat 1 tablespoon oil and fry tamarind paste for 1 minute over low heat. Dish out, add water and mix well. Strain tamarind juice.

Heat 1 tablespoon oil and fry **A** over low heat until fragrant. Add strained tamarind juice and water and bring to a boil. Stir in **B**. Remove from heat and stir in ground peanuts.

Garnish vegetables with shallot and garlic crisps. Serve with sauce or pour sauce over vegetables and mix well just before serving.

Pecal (h 96)

Soto Ayam

A lovely dish for a cold day. Replace rice cakes with scalded noodles and you'll have *Mee Soto*.

Preparation: 45 minutes
Cooking: (rice cakes) 30 minutes
           (25 burgers) 20 minutes
           (soup) 45 minutes

Rice Cakes - see *Nasi Himpit* (p 87).

600 g potatoes, boiled and mashed

300 g beef, minced

1 tablespoon pepper

1½ teaspoons salt

10 shallots, sliced and lightly browned in oil

2 eggs, beaten

a little flour

oil for shallow frying

A

7½ cm stick cinnamon

5 sections of a star anise

2 cardamoms

10 black peppercorns

1 heaped teaspoon white peppercorns

1 teaspoon coriander powder (p 43)

½ teaspoon fennel

½ teaspoon cummin

15 cups water

5 cm ginger, crushed lightly

4 cloves garlic

1½ kg chicken, halved

2 teaspoons salt

2 tablespoons oil reserved from frying shallots (see below)

450 g beansprouts, tailed and scalded in boiling water for 1 minute

300 g shallots, sliced and fried crisp in oil
(reserve 2 tablespoons of this oil)

4 sprigs Chinese celery (p 100), chopped

40 bird chillies (p 94), ground, and

3 tablespoons light soya sauce, combined

(cont'd on p 100)

Chinese celery and Chinese parsely (coriander, p 43)
Local or Chinese celery is smaller and more pungent than large white celery. It can be substituted with the leaves and top portion of the centre of a large celery.

Put potatoes and minced beef in a bowl and mix well with pepper, salt and fried shallots. Stir in eggs. Form mixture into 5 cm diameter patties with wet hands. Roll lightly in a little plain flour and shallow fry in a little oil for about 5 minutes or until cooked. When cool, quarter each burger.

Tie up **A** in a piece of clean cloth with a thick string. Crush bag of spices lightly with a pestle. Prick bag with a skewer.

Put water, bag of spices, ginger and garlic in a large pot and bring to a slow boil. Put in chicken and simmer, covered, for 30 minutes or until chicken is tender. Add salt. Remove scum from soup and add 2 tablespoons of oil reserved from frying shallots. Remove chicken and tear meat into small pieces. Place in a serving dish.

To serve, put a few rice cubes, some beansprouts, burgers and chicken in a serving bowl. Top with hot chicken soup and garnish with shallot crisps and Chinese celery. Serve hot, and if desired, with a small dish of bird chillies and light soya sauce.

Mee Rebus

Preparation: 1 hour
Cooking: 30 minutes

300 g beef
8 tablespoons oil

A
20 dried chillies (p 94), seeded
30 shallots
4 cloves garlic
5 cm turmeric root
2½ cm galingale (lengkuas)
40 black peppercorns
2 tablespoons preserved soya beans (p 19)

12 cups coconut milk, from 1 grated coconut
900 g sweet potatoes, steamed
600 g fresh yellow noodles, scalded in boiling water
300 g beansprouts, tailed and scalded in boiling water

5 hardboiled eggs, quartered
4 stalks spring onion, chopped
5 green chillies, sliced
10 small limes, halved
prawn crisps, crushed lightly

Grind **A**. Cut beef into thin slices.

Heat oil in a *kuali* and fry **A** until fragrant and oil separates. Put in beef and fry for 2 minutes, then pour in blended ingredients. Bring to a slow boil, lower heat and simmer for 5-10 minutes. Add rice flour mixed with a little water to thicken gravy, then add sugar and salt. When it comes to a boil again, turn off heat. Reheat again just before serving.

To serve, put some noodles and beansprouts into individual serving bowls. Pour hot gravy over and garnish with hardboiled eggs, spring onions, green chillies, limes and prawn crisps.

Prawn Crisps

6 tablespoons plain flour, sifted
9 tablespoons water
½ teaspoon salt
1 tablespoon ground prawns
oil for deep frying

Mix flour with water into a smooth batter. Stir in salt and ground prawns.

Heat oil in a *kuali* until hot. Spoon a tablespoon of batter into hot oil, carefully spreading batter out. Fry over medium heat until golden brown. Drain on absorbent paper and keep in an air-tight container until serving time.

Something from everything: (clockwise from left) *Mee Siam Kering* (p 104), Chinese Ladle Cake (p 42), Orange and Lime Chiffon Cake (p 209), *Nyonya Kuih Mah Chee* (p 44), *Samosa* (p 190), Shell Curry Puff (p 235), Nonya Meat Cake (p 43), *Lempar Udang* (p 147), *Ayam Pulut Panggang* (p 145), *Otak-Otak* (p 92), and (in centre) *Abok-Abok Sago* (p 140).

Mee Siam Kering

A variation of *mee siam* that's great for parties as there is no mess.

Preparation: 30 minutes
Cooking: 20 minutes

600 g rice vermicelli
¾ cup oil
20 shallots, sliced
2 firm soyabean cakes, cut into small cubes
1 onion, ground
A
15 dried chillies (p 94), soaked
3 tablespoons dried prawns
300 g small prawns, shelled
240 g beef, thinly sliced
2 teaspoons salt
2 eggs, beaten lightly
3 stalks mustard greens (choy sum), stems smashed lightly, cut into 5 cm lengths (separate stems and leaves)
300 g beansprouts
10-12 stalks Chinese chives, cut into 2½ cm lengths
3 sprigs Chinese celery (p 104), chopped
3 red chillies, sliced
3 green chillies, sliced
10 small limes, halved

Soak vermicelli in water for 10 minutes until soft. Drain in a colander. Grind **A** finely.

Heat oil in a *kuali* and fry sliced shallots until golden brown. Remove with a perforated ladle and leave aside. Fry soyabean cakes until lightly browned. Remove and leave aside. Fry ground onion in the same oil until fragrant, add **A** and stir fry until fragrant. Put in prawns, then add beef and salt.

Pour in beaten eggs and quickly stir fry. Add mustard green, stems first then leaves. Stir fry, then add fried soyabean cakes. Put in rice vermicelli and mix well.

Add beansprouts and Chinese chives and fry briskly for 2 minutes. Lastly, add half the chopped Chinese celery. Place on a large dish and garnish with remaining Chinese celery, red and green chillies, limes and shallot crisps.

Laksa Lemak

This is a rich curry noodle fragrant with spices that is known as *laksa* in the south and *curry mee* in the north of Malaysia. The right combination of root spices with a *lemak* (rich) coconut milk gravy is essential. This recipe has the right blend that will certainly please the most discerning palate for *laksa*. You can replace the prawns with chicken, if you like.

Preparation: 25 minutes
Cooking: 25 minutes

1¼ cups oil

A
600 g shallots
5 cm turmeric root
40 dried chillies (p 94), soaked
6 red chillies
4 cm x 5 cm dried shrimp paste (belacan)
10 candlenuts
6 stalks lemon grass
2½ cm x 5 cm galingale (lengkuas)
60 g dried prawns

1 kg large prawns, shells retained
16 cups coconut milk, from 3 grated coconuts
3 fish cakes, sliced
3 teaspoons salt
1½ kg fresh or 2 packets dried thick rice vermicelli, scalded and drained

600 g beansprouts, tailed and scalded
2 cucumbers, peeled and shredded
2 bunches mint leaves

(cont'd on p106)

Grind **A**. Heat oil in a *kuali* and fry **A** until fragrant and oil appears on surface. Put in large prawns and stir fry for 3 minutes until prawns are cooked. Dish out the prawns only and leave aside. This will prevent prawns from being overcooked. Pour in coconut milk and bring to a boil. Put in fish cake slices. When gravy boils again, add prawns and salt.

To serve, put a little thick rice vermicelli into individual serving bowls. Garnish with beansprouts, cucumber and mint leaves. Pour hot gravy with prawns and fish slices over this.

Assam Laksa

'Sour *laksa* is very popular in the north of Malaysia and is one of the many dishes that Penang is famous for. The tangy taste of tamarind blends well with the aromatic polygonum leaves and ginger flowers. However, it may take a little getting used to. *Assam laksa* gourmets swear that using an earthern pot improves the flavour of the gravy. And it is certainly one dish where the taste improves the next day.

Preparation: 1½ hours
Cooking: 30 minutes

4 tablespoons tamarind paste mixed with 1 cup water, strained

A
40 dried chillies (p 94), soaked
6 slices galingale (lengkuas)
1¼ cm x 2½ cm x 5 cm dried shrimp paste (belacan), ground
3 stalks lemon grass
180 g shallots

6 cups water
10-12 sprigs polygonum (daun kesum) leaves
3-4 wild ginger flowers, buds split and stems smashed
4 pieces dried tamarind skin (assam gelugor)
1¾ kg wolf herring (ikan parang), steamed and flaked
2 tablespoons sugar
salt to taste
600 g fresh thick rice vermicelli, parboiled

B
½ pineapple, sliced and cut into strips
1 cucumber, skinned and shredded
½ head lettuce, shredded finely
1 onion, sliced finely
3 red chillies, seeded and sliced
1 sprig mint leaves
6-8 small limes, halved
black shrimp paste (heiko), mixed with a little water

Assam gelugor
These are slices of dried tamarind fruit that are used for their sourness. Substitute with dried tamarind pulp, if unavailable.

To make tamarind water from the pulp, soak 1 heaped tablespoon of pulp in the required amount of water for about 5 minutes. Squeeze with your fingers to extract the juice and strain any fibrous matter, stones or skins from the juice.

Put tamarind juice, **A** and water to boil in an earthern pot. Add polygonum leaves, wild ginger flowers and dried tamarind skin and simmer over low heat for 15 minutes.

Add flaked fish, sugar and salt to taste. Simmer for a few minutes. Remove polygonum leaves, wild ginger flowers and dried tamarind skin just before dishing out gravy.

(cont'd on p 108)

The sweet and sour of Malay cooking:
(top) *Assam Laksa* (p 107), (right) *Mee Rebus* (p 101),
(at left, top) *Bubur Terigu* with *Pulut* (p 112), (left) *Pulut
Hitam* (p 111) and (right) *Cendol* (p 109).

To serve, put some noodles in individual bowls and garnish with a little of **B**. Pour boiling gravy over noodles and add 1 teaspoon black shrimp paste. Serve immediately.

Cendol

The *cendol* man used to be a popular sight along alleys, and an especially welcome one on hot days. You can still get *cendol* in the modern hawker centres and even hotel coffee-houses, but it's never the same. Try this and relive the old days or gain a new experience!

Preparation: 1 hour
Cooking: 40 minutes

10 *pandan leaves, cut into 2½ cm pieces*
1 *cup water*
a few drops green colouring
1 *packet (85 g) green bean flour (p 44)*
1 *cup extra water*
1 *teaspoon vanilla essence*

A
360 *g palm sugar* (gula melaka), *cut into small pieces*
120 *g granulated sugar*
1 *cup water*
3 *pandan leaves*

2 *white coconuts, grated*
4 *cups cool boiled water*
¼ *teaspoon salt*

Blend pandan leaves in a blender with l cup water. Strain with a fine strainer into a saucepan and add a few drops of green colouring. Bring to a boil.

Blend green bean flour with the extra cup of water and gradually stir into boiling pandan juice with a wooden spoon. Stir continuously until mixture is transparent and thick.

Prepare a basin of ice-cold water with a few cubes of ice in it. Place a *cendol* frame over the basin and put cooked green bean flour, a little at a time, onto the frame. Press into little droplets of *cendol*, using a wooden spoon. Refrigerate for l0 minutes, then drain and return to the refrigerator.

The Malays have lovely sweet desserts that are great after a chilli hot meal. Try one of the few here. Just keep stock of the basic ingredients in your kitchen and you'll be able to prepare one in a jiffy. All you'll need is the coconut milk.

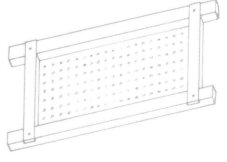

(cont'd on p 110)

Put **A** in a saucepan and boil till sugar dissolves. Strain, allow to cool, then refrigerate.

Mix coconut with cool water. Squeeze and strain to obtain coconut milk. Stir in salt.

To serve, put 3 tablespoons *cendol* in each serving bowl. Pour in coconut milk and add palm syrup to taste. Top with ice shavings.

Bubur Cha-Cha

Preparation: 30 minutes
Cooking: 30 minutes

450 g sweet potatoes
450 g yam
¼ teaspoon salt
½ cup thick coconut milk and
6 cups thin coconut milk, from 1½ grated white coconuts
450 g sugar
4 pandan leaves, knotted
180 g tapioca flour, sifted
½ cup boiling hot water
2 drops red colouring mixed with 1 teaspoon water
2 drops green colouring mixed with 1 teaspoon water

Skin and cut sweet potatoes and yam into 2½ cm diamond-shaped pieces. Steam sweet potatoes and yam for 15 minutes. Leave aside.

Add salt to thick coconut milk and keep aside. Do not refrigerate.

In a large saucepan, boil thin coconut milk, sugar and pandan leaves. When sugar has dissolved, remove from heat. Discard pandan leaves. Allow sweet coconut milk to cool.

Put half the tapioca flour in a bowl, add ¼ cup boiling hot water and red colouring. Mix into a paste and knead into a dough. Repeat procedure with remaining half of tapioca flour and green colouring.

On a board lightly floured with tapioca flour, roll dough into thin strips and cut into small diamond-shaped pieces. Boil half a saucepan of water, then drop in tapioca pieces. When the pieces float, scoop out with a perforated ladle and drop them into a bowl of cold water.

To serve, put 2-3 tablespoons of sweet potato and yam and 1 tablespoon of tapioca pieces into individual serving bowls. Top with cool sweet coconut milk and 1 tablespoon thick coconut milk. Add crushed ice and serve immediately.

Bubur Pulut Hitam

Preparation: 15 minutes
Cooking: 1 hour

240 g black glutinous rice (pulut hitam), *washed and drained*
60 g glutinous rice (pulut), *washed and drained*
7 cups water
2 pandan leaves, knotted
½ cup sugar
pinch of salt
½ tablespoon tapioca flour or cornflour combined with 2 tablespoons water to form a paste
½ cup thick coconut milk, from ½ grated white coconut
pinch of salt

Put rice in a pot with water and pandan leaves and bring to a boil. Reduce heat to low, remove pandan leaves and simmer for 45 minutes until liquid is thick. Add sugar and simmer for 10 minutes. Add salt and thickening. Remove from heat.

Serve in small bowls topped with 1-2 tablespoons thick coconut milk.

White (*pulut*) and black (*pulut hitam*) glutinous rice.

Bubur Kacang Hijau

Preparation: 15 minutes
Cooking: 40 minutes

120 g green/mung beans, washed and drained
5 cups water
2 pandan leaves, knotted
120 g sugar (for more fragrance, use palm sugar)
pinch of salt
½ cup thick coconut milk, from ½ grated coconut, combined with a pinch of salt

Put green beans in a pot with water and pandan leaves. Bring to a boil. Remove pandan leaves and continue simmering over low heat for 30 minutes until beans are soft. Add sugar and salt.

Serve in small bowls topped with 1-2 tablespoons of thick coconut milk.

Bubur Terigu with Pulut

Preparation: 15 minutes
Cooking: 1 hour

120 g wheat corn (terigu), washed and drained
60 g glutinous rice (pulut), washed and drained
7 cups water
2 pandan leaves, knotted
180 g sugar
pinch of salt
½ cup thick coconut milk, from ½ grated white coconut, combined with a pinch of salt
palm sugar (gula melaka) syrup

Put wheat corn and rice in a pot with water and *pandan* leaves and bring to a boil. Remove *pandan* leaves. Reduce heat to low and simmer for 45 minutes until soft and liquid is thick (when the wheat corn and glutinous rice is throughly cooked, the mixture will turn starchy and thicken). Stir in sugar and salt.

Serve in small bowls topped with 1-2 tablespoons of thick coconut milk and palm syrup.

(from top) green/mung beans (*kacang hijau*), pearl sago, wheat corn (*terigu*).

KUIH-MUIH

Kuih-muih spread:
(clockwise from top right)
Kuih Koci (p 139), *Kuih
Pelita* (p 118), *Onde-Onde*
(p 115), Sticky Rice with
Mango (p 118), *Kuih Pandan*
(p 114), *Kuih Talam* (p 142)
and *Kuih Serimuka* (p 123).

Kuih Pandan

Preparation: 20 minutes
Steaming: 1 hour
Makes: approximately 30 pieces

Pandan leaf
The *pandan* leaf (sometimes referred to as screwpine in English) is an aromatic member of the pandanus family. Tying each leaf tied in a knot, they are very often added to Malay and Nyonya rice and sweet dishes, while the juice is extracted for *kuih*s and desserts. To obtain pandan juice, pound and squeeze the leaves or liquidise cut pieces of the leaves with a little water.

Pandan leaves are used for their special fragrance and *kuih* made with coconut milk simply will not be the same without these wonderfully fragrant leaves.

5 pandan leaves, washed and cut into small pieces
1 ½ cups coconut milk, from ½ grated coconut
60 g sugar
2-3 drops green colouring
¼ teaspoon salt
90 g rice flour, sifted
30 g tapioca flour, sifted
90 g grated white coconut, from a young coconut mixed with a pinch of salt

Put pandan leaves into a blender and blend until fine with ¹/₂ cup of the coconut milk. Strain into a large mixing bowl. Add remaining coconut milk and stir in sugar, green colouring and salt. When sugar is dissolved, add sifted rice and tapioca flours. Stir until smooth. Strain mixture to remove lumps, if any.

Steam a 17 cm square baking tin or dish for 5 minutes. Stir flour mixture thoroughly, then pour into baking tin or dish. Continue stirring mixture for 5-10 minutes. Cover lid of steamer with greaseproof paper or a large dry tea towel to prevent water from dripping onto the *kuih*. Lower heat to moderate and continue steaming for 50 minutes to 1 hour.

Cool thoroughly, then cut into 4 cm squares. Roll in grated coconut mixed with salt.

Onde-Onde

This great favourite is also known as *Kuih Buah Melaka*. I've given two recipes here. The first makes firm *onde-onde* with a sticky 'glutinous' bite. The second, with the addition of sweet potato, makes softer *onde-onde*. They also keep well for a whole day without turning hard, that is if they are not all gone by then! I never seem to make enough.

It is essential to seal the balls of dough. Otherwise, the palm sugar will ooze out discolouring the *onde-onde* when boiled. And to ensure that the filled *onde-onde* does not dry up, cover with a tea towel as you are making them. If they should dry and fine cracks appear, moisten with a little water and seal again.

Preparation: 20 minutes
Cooking: 10 minutes
Makes: 38-40

---
240 g glutinous rice flour

¾ cup boiling hot water combined with 1 tablespoon pandan juice and a few drops green colouring
---
120 g palm sugar (gula melaka), *cut into small pieces*

½ grated white coconut mixed with pinch of salt

Sift glutinous rice flour into a bowl. Add combined boiling hot water, pandan juice and green colouring. Mix well and knead into a firm lump of dough.

Form into marble-size balls. Flatten each ball lightly and fill with 1 or 2 pieces of palm sugar. Press edges together and shape into small balls.

Boil half a saucepan of water, put in the glutinous rice balls, a few at a time. When cooked, glutinous rice balls will rise to the surface. Dish out with a perforated ladle and roll in grated coconut mixed with salt.

Ever-Soft Onde-Onde

Preparation: 30 minutes
Cooking: 30 minutes
Makes: 38-40

---
250 g peeled sweet potato, cut into wedges and rinsed in salt water to prevent discolouration
---
350 g glutinous rice flour combined with
1 tablespoon pandan juice and a few drops green colouring
¼ teaspoon salt
---
150 g palm sugar (gula melaka), cut into small pieces
½ grated white coconut mixed with pinch of salt

Steam sweet potato over rapidly boiling water for 15 minutes until soft. Mash well with a potato masher while still hot.

Sift glutinous rice into a mixing bowl and add enough water to bind into a ball of dough. Add hot mashed sweet potato and knead well. It should be soft in texture but not sticky.

Divide into walnut-size portions. Roll each into a round ball. Flatten slightly and fill with a teaspoonful of palm sugar. Seal well. Drop into boiling water. As soon as they float to the surface, remove with a perforated ladle. Roll in grated coconut mixed with salt.

Puteri Berendam

Very much like *Onde-Onde* except this is served with a sauce. The literal meaning is 'princess swimming'.

Preparation: 15 minutes
Cooking: 20 minutes
Makes: 24

60 g palm sugar (gula melaka), *chopped*
¼ cup water
pinch of salt
120 g grated white coconut
150 g glutinous rice flour
1 cup water
a few drops green colouring
1 ½ cups thick coconut milk, from 1 grated coconut
3 tablespoons sugar
¼ teaspoon salt
½ tablespoon flour
3 pandan leaves, knotted

Put palm sugar, water and salt into a small saucepan over low heat and stir until palm sugar dissolves. Strain into a *kuali*, add grated coconut and fry till evenly coated with palm syrup. Dish out and cool filling.

Sift glutinous rice flour into a bowl, add water and knead into a firm dough together with green colouring. Form into small marble-size balls. Flatten each ball lightly and fill with a teaspoonful of filling. Press edges together and shape into small balls.

Boil half a saucepan of water and put in glutinous rice balls, a few at a time. As soon as they float to the surface, remove with a perforated ladle.

Mix coconut milk, sugar, salt and flour in a saucepan until smooth. Put in pandan leaves and bring to a boil, stirring continuously. Add glutinous rice balls and simmer for a few minutes until coconut milk thickens. Serve hot in small dishes.

Glutinous Roll with Kaya

Preparation: 20 minutes
Cooking: 10 minutes
Steaming: 2 hours
Makes: approximately 32 pieces

4 cups thick coconut milk, from 3 grated coconuts
1 ½ teaspoons salt
1 kg glutinous rice, washed and drained
10 pieces (18 cm x 23 cm) banana leaves, scalded

Put thick coconut milk and salt in a large saucepan and bring to a slow boil over low heat. Add glutinous rice and stir for 10-15 minutes until almost dry. Cover saucepan and cook over low heat for 20 minutes until glutinous rice is half-cooked. Cool.

Put 3-4 tablespoons of half-cooked glutinous rice in the centre of each banana leaf. Roll into a long roll approximately 4 cm in diameter. Twist and tie the two ends securely with strong strings.

Place glutinous rice rolls in a steamer and steam for 2 hours over low heat. Cool. Discard banana leaves and cut into 2½ cm thick slices. Serve with *kaya*.

Kaya

A wonderful egg-based custard spread.

Preparation: 30 minutes
Cooking: 55 minutes

1½ cups thick coconut milk, from grated whites of 3 coconuts
10 eggs
600 g coarse sugar
1 teaspoon vanilla essence
3 pandan leaves, knotted

In a saucepan lightly beat eggs with sugar. Place over low heat, stirring continously for about 10 minutes to dissolve sugar. Remove pandan leaves.

Add thick coconut milk and strain mixture into a heatproof container. Steam over rapidly boiling water stirring with a wooden spoon for approximately 45 minutes until the egg mixture turns into a thick custard mixture. Cool and bottle in jam jars.

Sticky Rice with Mango

Preparation: 20 minutes
Steaming: 25 minutes

480 g glutinous rice, soaked in water overnight and drained

A

1 cup thick coconut milk, from 1 grated coconut
20 g sugar and ¼ teaspoon salt

B

2 cups thick coconut milk, from 1 grated coconut,
combined with ¼ teaspoon salt

mango slices

Place rice in a steaming tray. Steam over rapidly boiling water for 15 minutes. Pour **A** over hot rice. Cover and steam for a further 10 minutes. Cool.

Bring **B** to a slow boil over low heat. Allow coconut sauce to cool before serving.

To serve, spoon portion of glutinous rice onto a serving dish. Arrange mango slices over rice and top with a generous serving of coconut sauce.

Kuih Pelita / Tepung Pelita

Kuih Pelita, served well-chilled, makes a super tea treat or after-lunch dessert. There is a pleasing charm at the sight of the dessert neatly encased in banana leaves. And the fragrance of coconut milk and pandan enhanced with banana leaves makes this one of my firm favourites. I usually gorge them with a greed that far surpasses appetite.

Preparation: 50 minutes
Steaming: 15 minutes
Makes: 34

34-36 pieces (2 cm x 10 cm) banana leaves
granulated sugar

225 g rice flour
60 g sugar
8 pandan leaves, cut into small pieces
3¼ cups thick coconut milk (for coconut topping) and
7½ cups thin coconut milk, from 3 grated coconuts
¼ teaspoon salt
1 teaspoon vanilla essence
few drops of green colouring

60 g rice flour
30 g sugar
3¼ cups reserved thick coconut milk
¾ teaspoon salt

Scald banana leaves and dry with a tea towel. Fold into boat shapes and secure by stapling the two folded ends. Fill each boat with 1 tablespoon of granulated sugar and arrange boats in neat rows, one against the other. This will help the boats keep their shape when filled.

Sift 225 g rice flour into a large saucepan and add sugar. Put pandan leaves with half of the thin coconut milk and blend in an electric blender. Strain mixture. Gradually add to rice flour together with remaining coconut milk and mix well with salt, vanilla essence and a few drops of green colouring if you prefer a greener layer. Bring mixture to a slow boil, stirring all the time with a wooden spoon until it thickens and turns glossy and smooth.

Fill boats with 2 tablespoons of cooked mixture while still piping hot. When this is done, proceed to cook coconut topping.

Sift remaining 60 g rice flour into a saucepan, add sugar and gradually stir in thick coconut milk together with salt. Cook mixture over medium heat, stirring all the time until thick, glossy and smooth. Put 1 tablespoon of this mixture, while still hot over the green layer.

Steam over rapidly boiling water for 15 minutes. Allow to cool thoroughly before serving.

Pandan Flavoured Kuih Koswee

Don't attempt to steam the *kuih* in double-tier steamers as water tends to drip onto the filled cups resulting in soggy-topped *kuih*.

Preparation: 20 minutes
Steaming: 25 minutes
Makes : 50

420 g granulated sugar
2 cups water
8 pandan leaves, cut into small pieces
1 ¼ cups water
200 g rice flour, sifted
⅔ cup water
120 g sago flour, sifted
⅛ teaspoon borax (pangsar)
1 dessertspoon alkaline water (kansui)
2-3 drops green colouring
grated white coconut, from half a young coconut
pinch of salt

Put sugar and water in a saucepan and bring to a slow boil to dissolve sugar. Allow to cool and leave aside.

Put pandan leaves and water into a blender and blend into a fine pulp. Squeeze and strain to obtain juice. Leave aside.

Sift rice flour into a mixing bowl and add ⅔ cup water. Mix to form a dough. Add sago flour and gradually add strained pandan juice, stirring until smooth. Stir in borax, alkaline water and green colouring. Lastly, pour in cooled syrup and mix well.

Steam 25 small Chinese teacups for 5 minutes. Stir flour mixture thoroughly. For easier filling, pour mixture into a large measuring jug with a beak. Fill ¾ of each teacup with mixture. Give each and every filled teacup a quick stir with a chopstick. Cover lid with a dry tea towel to prevent steam from entering the mixture. Steam over rapidly boiling water for 25 minutes.

Mix grated coconut with salt. Remove *kuih* from mould when cooled. Roll in coconut topping. Repeat steaming again with remaining mixture.

Lebat Ubi Kayu (Grated Tapioca Wrapped in Banana Leaves)

Preparation: 45 minutes
Steaming: 30 minutes
Makes: 20

2 kg tapioca, cleaned
approximately 3 cups water
600 g palm sugar (gula melaka)*, chopped into*
small pieces boiled with ½ cup water, strained
6 pandan leaves
360 g granulated sugar
½ grated white coconut
½ cup thick coconut milk, from ½ grated coconut
½ teaspoon salt
20 pieces (20 cm x 22 cm) banana leaves, scalded

Cut tapioca into small pieces. Place in blender with enough water and blend until fine.

Using a fine piece of muslin cloth, put a ladleful of tapioca pulp and squeeze until dry. Do this over a deep bowl to collect the liquid. When this process is completed, leave the yellow liquid to settle undisturbed for at least 30 minutes. Then, carefully pour away the yellow liquid taking care not to disturb the white starch which has settled at the bottom of the bowl. (The Chinese believe that the yellow liquid is 'windy' and weakening.)

In a separate bowl, combine the tapioca pulp with granulated sugar, grated coconut, the settled white starch, thick coconut milk and salt. Stir in strained palm sugar syrup and mix well.

Place 3 heaped dessertspoons of tapioca mixture in the centre of each banana leaf. Fold leaf to overlap lengthwise over mixture and tuck the other ends under. Repeat with remaining mixture. Steam over rapidly boiling water for 30 minutes. Serve cold.

Pulut Serikaya (2)

Preparation: 30 minutes
Steaming: 1 hour 10 minutes
Makes: approximately
24 pieces

30 g cornflour
1 cup reserved thick coconut milk
3 eggs
180 g castor sugar
350 g glutinous rice, washed
1 cup thick coconut milk (for *serikaya*) and 1 ½ cups thin coconut milk (for *pulut* base), from 1 ½ grated coconuts
½ teaspoon salt
3 pandan leaves, knotted

Mix the cornflour with thick coconut milk. Stir eggs and sugar gently together until sugar dissolves. Do not beat. Slowly stir in combined coconut milk and cornflour mixture. Strain through a strainer. Leave aside.

Prepare *pulut* base as for first recipe.

Pour prepared *serikaya* topping over rice. Reduce heat to low and steam for 45 minutes until topping is set. Remove to cool before cutting into slices.

Pulut Serikaya

Two recipes for a favourite Malay teatime snack. The first recipe has a richer topping than the second.

Preparation: 30 minutes
Steaming: 32 minutes
Makes: approximately 24 pieces

7 eggs
450 g sugar
5 tablespoons plain flour
½ teaspoon yellow colouring
2 tablespoons rose water or 2 teaspoons vanilla essence
1 ½ cups reserved thick coconut milk
900 g glutinuous rice
1 teaspoon salt
1 ½ cups thick coconut milk (for serikaya*) and 1 cup thin coconut milk (for* pulut *base), from 2 grated coconuts*

Mix eggs with sugar and flour until smooth. Add yellow colouring, rose water or vanilla essence and thick coconut milk. Leave aside.

Soak glutinuous rice for 2 hours. Drain and put in a 25 cm cake pan. Mix in salt and thin coconut milk. Steam over rapidly boiling water for 10 minutes. Press rice down firmly with the back of a spoon and steam for a further 10 minutes.

Pour prepared *serikaya* topping over steamed rice. If mixture is lumpy, strain over rice. Steam over medium heat for 12 minutes. Cool before cutting into slices.

Kuih Serimuka

Preparation: 30 minutes
Steaming: 45 minutes
Makes: 24 pieces

4 eggs
180 g sugar
80 g plain flour
30 g tapioca flour
1 ½ cups thick coconut milk, from 1 small grated coconut
¼ cup pandan juice
a few drops green colouring
½ teaspoon vanilla essence
½ coconut, grated
1 ½ cups water
480 g glutinous rice
1 ¼ teaspoons salt

Stir eggs and sugar together in a bowl. Do not beat. Sift in plain and tapioca flours. Mix well. Gradually pour in coconut milk, pandan juice, green colouring and essence. Strain to remove lumps. Leave topping aside.

Blend coconut and water. Squeeze and strain to obtain coconut milk. Wash glutinous rice and put in a 25-27 cm round pan. Pour in enough coconut milk to cover the rice. Stir in salt.

Steam for 20-25 minutes. When cooked, press down firmly with the back of a spoon. Pour in prepared topping and steam for a further 20 minutes over medium heat.

Kuih Wajek
(Glutinous Rice Pudding)

Preparation: 20 minutes
Steaming: 1 hour
Cooking: 15 minutes
Makes: 36

½ cup water
300 g palm sugar (gula melaka), *cut into small pieces*
60 g granulated sugar
3 pandan leaves, knotted
600 g glutinous rice, soaked overnight
pinch of salt
2 cups thick coconut milk, from 2 grated coconuts

Put water, palm sugar, granulated sugar and pandan leaves in a saucepan and stir over low heat until sugar dissolves. Strain syrup.

Line the base of a steaming tray with a piece of muslin and place a few extra strips of pandan leaves on the cloth. Spread glutinous rice over pandan leaves and steam for 45 minutes.

Add salt to coconut milk. Mix steamed rice with coconut milk and strained syrup and cook over low heat, stirring continuously till mixture becomes thick and a rich oily brown.

Spread mixture on an 18 cm x 28 cm tray and allow to cool and harden. Cut into 4 cm squares.

Kuih Bingka Telur

Preparation: 20 minutes
Baking: 1 hour
Oven setting (first 45 minutes): 175 °C
(last 15 minutes): 150 °C

6 eggs
270 g granulated sugar
195 g plain flour, sifted
30 g melted butter
pinch of salt
1 teaspoon vanilla essence
4 cups coconut milk, from 3 grated coconuts
2-3 drops yellow colouring

Line the base of a 22 cm square cake tin with greased greaseproof paper.

Lightly stir eggs and sugar together. Add sifted flour gradually to egg mixture and mix well. Stir in melted butter, salt, vanilla essence and coconut milk a little at a time. Add yellow colouring and strain mixture into the prepared tin.

Bake in a moderate oven for 45 minutes. Lower temperature and bake a further 15 minutes until set. Cool in the tin then cut into 4 cm cubes.

Kuih Koleh-Koleh Kacang

If this is one of your favourite treats, as it is mine, it's worth the effort to wash as much as 2-3 kilograms of green mung beans during your spare time, pan-fry or oven-roast till dry, then send to the mill for grinding. It keeps well for months especially in the refrigerator. But you can use green bean flour, if available. Simply sift flour and stir in coconut milk without adding water.

To thoroughly remove small stones and grit from beans, wash and scoop beans with fingers into a separate container instead of draining water away from the pan. This way the heavier sand and grit will remain at the bottom of the pan. Do this several times.

Preparation: 15 minutes
Cooking: 1 hour 10 minutes
Makes: approximately 32 pieces

300 g green/mung beans, soaked for at least 2 hours, preferably overnight
4 cups water
3 cups thick coconut milk, from 1½ grated coconuts
450 g palm sugar (gula melaka), cut into small pieces
½ cup water
2 pandan leaves
coconut residue crisps

Wash green beans and put in a pressure cooker with 4 cups water. Cook for 20 minutes. Put in a blender with coconut milk and blend until fine. For easier and finer blending, do this a third at a time. If blender is not turning well, add a little extra coconut milk.

Melt palm sugar with water over heat, stirring frequently. Strain into blended mixture. Mix well.

Pour mixture into a *kuali*, add pandan leaves and stir continuously with a wooden spatula over low heat for 15 minutes or until it becomes a thick paste. Do not allow mixture to stick to bottom of *kuali*. When paste is thick enough, make a figure 8 with the spatula. If it holds well, paste is of right consistency. Discard pandan leaves.

Spoon into an 18 cm x 27 cm shallow tin and smooth surface while still hot with a piece of banana leaf or a butter knife. Sprinkle with prepared coconut residue crisps. Leave to cool thoroughly before cutting.

Tahi Minyak (Coconut Residue Crisps for topping)

Coconut reside crisps when drained from oil and cooled can be stored in an air-tight container for as long as a week without refrigeration. A tablespoon or two of this added to sambal prawns with slightly thicker gravy will impart a delightful flavour.

1 cup thick coconut milk, from 1 grated coconut

Put thick coconut milk into a *kuali* and stir over low heat with a wooden spatula for 30-35 minutes. Oil will separate from coconut residue. Continue stirring until coconut residue turns a rich brown. Remove from heat and drain.

Kuih Bakar Jagung

Preparation: 15 minutes
Baking: 50 minutes
Makes: 21

1 can (450 g) sweetcorn
2 ⅔ cups coconut milk, from 1½ grated coconuts
240 g flour
195 g granulated sugar
4 eggs, beaten lightly with a fork
1 tablespoon margarine, melted
1 teaspoon vanilla essence

Put sweetcorn and a little of the coconut milk in a blender and blend until fine. Leave aside.

Sift flour into a mixing bowl, add sugar and stir in remaining coconut milk a little at a time until smooth. If batter is lumpy, put through a strainer. Stir in eggs, blended sweetcorn, melted margarine and vanilla essence.

Grease individual *kuih bakar* patty tins with margarine. Fill patty tins with sweetcorn batter and bake in a moderate oven for 50 minutes until top is lightly browned.

Allow to cool before turning out. Loosen *kuih* by running a round-bladed knife along edge of patty tin. The *kuih* will sink slightly in the centre as it cools.

If *kuih bakar* patty tins are not available, use normal cup cake patty tins which are slightly shallower. These moulds are also used for *Kuih Cara Manis* (p 133) and *Kuih Cara Berlauk* (p 134).

Kuih Nagasari

Preparation: 30 minutes
Cooking: 30 minutes
Makes: 16

240 g rice flour
2 cups water
3½ cups coconut milk, from 1 grated coconut
2 pandan leaves, knotted
½ teaspoon salt
16 pieces (18 cm x 15cm) banana leaves, scalded
8 small ripe bananas (pisang rajah), *peeled and halved lengthwise*

Sift rice flour into a bowl, add water and blend mixture until smooth. Place coconut milk, pandan leaves and salt in a saucepan and bring to a slow boil. Add rice batter to coconut milk and stir with a wooden spoon for approximately 5 minutes until mixture turns into a smooth paste. Remove from heat.

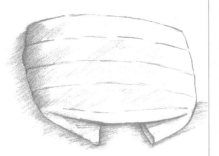

Place a dessertspoonful of cooked mixture in the centre of each banana leaf. Fold one side of banana leaf to flatten mixture into a small rectangle. Top with a piece of banana and cover with another spoonful of dough mixture. Fold banana leaf, overlapping lengthwise to cover mixture and tuck the other end under. Steam for 20 minutes and serve hot or cold.

Pengat

This is served either hot or cold for tea or as a sweet.

Preparation: 10 minutes
Cooking: 50 minutes
Serves: 6

700 g yam
1 cup thick coconut milk and 3 cups thin coconut milk, from 1 grated coconut
180 g palm sugar (gula melaka), *chopped*
90 g sugar
4 pandan leaves, knotted
4 medium bananas (pisang rajah)

Peel yam and cut into 3 portions. Steam over rapidly boiling water for 25 minutes. When cool, cut into $2^1/_2$ cm x 5 cm thick pieces.

Put thin coconut milk, palm sugar, sugar and pandan leaves in a sau pan, simmer and stir gently for 5 minutes to melt sugar. Add steamed yam and simmer gently for 15 minutes.

Peel and cut bananas at a slant into thick slices. Put into coconut milk mixture. When mixture boils, add thick coconut milk. Serve hot or cold.

Dodol

This is served usually during festive seasons such as *Hari Raya* and *Deepavali*. Roughly chopped cashewnuts can be added to the mixture for an even richer treat.

Preparation: 15 minutes
Cooking: $2^1/_2$ hours

1 kg glutinous rice flour
7 cups coconut milk, from 4 grated coconuts
700 g palm sugar (gula melaka), *chopped,*
240 g sugar and 1 cup water, boiled to dissolve sugar
3 pandan leaves, knotted

Put glutinous rice flour into a bowl and blend with coconut milk until smooth. Strain mixture into a large non-stick pan and cook over low heat, stirring all the time with a wooden spoon until mixture starts to thicken.

Strain palm sugar syrup into flour mixture and continue stirring for 2 hours until mixture turns into an oily lump of dark brown dough.

Put *dodol* into a *mengkuang* (pandan leave mat) basket. If this is not available put into two 15 cm x 25 cm ungreased pyrex dishes. Smooth surface with a plastic spatula and cool completely, preferably overnight, before cutting.

Mengkuang **basket**

Jemput Durian

A variation for lovers of the 'king of fruits'.

Preparation: 10 minutes
Cooking: 5 minutes
Makes: 20

A
90 g self-raising flour, 1 teaspoon baking powder, and 30 g cornflour, sifted

1 egg
15 g sugar
1/4 teaspoon salt

1/2 cup water or milk
180 g durian pulp from 1 small durian
oil for deep frying

Follow method as for *Jemput Pisang*. Add durian pulp instead of mashed bananas and mix well.

Jemput Pisang

This easy to make snack is very often found in Malay homes for tea or just as an anytime snack.

Preparation: 10 minutes
Cooking : 10 minutes
Makes: approximately 40

A
120 self-raising flour
30 g cornflour
1 teaspoon baking powder

2 eggs
30 g sugar
1/4 teaspoon salt

1/2 cup coconut milk, from 1/2 grated coconut
5 medium bananas (pisang rastali) *mashed*
oil for deep frying

Sift **A**. Whisk eggs and sugar until light and fluffy. Add salt and fold in **A** alternately with coconut milk. Add mashed bananas and mix well.

Heat oil in a *kuali* and fry tablespoonfuls of batter until golden brown. Drain well before serving.

Kuih Kodok
(Deep Fried Banana Balls)

A recipe to make use of over-ripe bananas.

Preparation: 15 minutes
Cooking: 5 minutes
Makes: approximately 20

A
195 g plain flour
½ teaspoon baking powder
pinch of salt
480 g peeled ripe bananas, mashed
oil for deep frying

Sift **A**. Add mashed bananas and mix well into a soft batter.

Heat oil in a *kuali* until hot and drop tablespoons of batter in. Remove with a perforated ladle when golden brown and drain on absorbent paper.

Kuih Lapis

Those sold in shops usually have different colours for the different layers requiring more work. So, in true Betty Yew-style, here is an easier method for just as tasty *kuih*.

Preparation: 20 minutes
Steaming: 30 minutes
Makes: 18

A
120 g rice flour
30 g green bean flour (p 44)
30 g tapioca flour
pinch of salt
1¼ cups coconut milk, from ½ grated coconut
180 g castor sugar
¼ teaspoon red colouring

Sift **A** into a mixing bowl. Add the coconut milk slowly and mix well. Put in the castor sugar and stir until sugar dissolves. Strain mixture and divide into two portions. Leave one portion uncoloured. Add red colouring to the other and mix well. (You can divide the mixture into as many portions as you like, colouring each a different colour if you want a multi-coloured *kuih*.)

Place a round 21 cm greased cake tin in steamer tray. Pour in ¾ cup of uncoloured batter into tray. Cover and steam over rapidly boiling water for 2½ minutes until cooked. Pour in ¾ cup of pink coloured batter and steam for 2½ minutes. Repeat procedure alternating uncoloured and coloured layers until batter is used up.

Remove from steamer and allow to cool. When cold cut into diamond-shaped pieces.

Kuih Cara Manis

This is known as *Kuih Bakar* in Singapore. No one seems to be able to explain the different names. The Malaysian name means 'sweet cakes' while the Singaporean means 'grilled cakes'.

Preparation: 15 minutes
Cooking: 1 hour
Makes: 60 small *kuih*

300 g flour
1¾ cups thick coconut milk, from 1 grated coconut
1 tablespoon pandan juice
2-3 drops green colouring
¼ teaspoon salt
2 eggs
castor sugar

Sift flour into a small mixing bowl. Stir in coconut milk a little at a time, together with pandan juice, colouring and salt. Lightly beat eggs with a fork and stir into flour mixture.

Grease egg-shaped *kuih cara* moulds (p 127) with a little butter and heat over very low heat. Instead of spooning batter into each individual mould, which would be time-consuming, pour batter into a measuring jug with a beak. This way, batter can be poured easily and quickly into moulds without spillage.

Fill each individual mould with batter and cook for approximately 8 minutes. When *kuih* is more than half-cooked, sprinkle a teaspoon of sugar evenly over surface of each. Remove with a small butter knife when completely cooked.

Kuih Cara Berlauk

The savoury version of the *Kuih Cara Manis* (p 133) is sometimes referred to as Malay quiche and is ideal for cocktail parties. Two fillings are given here – just double the batter if you intend making both.

Preparation: 20 minutes
Cooking: 1 hour
Makes: 60 small *kuih*

Meat Filling

Meat Filling
300 g beef, minced
3 tablespoons meat curry powder
2 tablespoons oil
2 onions, chopped finely
1 teaspoon salt

Season meat with curry powder.

Heat oil in a *kuali* and lightly brown onions. Add meat and salt. Stir fry till meat is cooked and dry. To prevent meat from sticking to pan, sprinkle in a little water while frying. Remove and leave aside.

Follow method for batter and *kuih*. You will need a bigger egg-shaped mould to sandwich the meat filling.

Prawn Filling
5 shallots, finely sliced
300 g small prawns shelled and cut into small pieces
½ teaspoon salt
¼ teaspoon pepper
2 tablespoons oil
2 red chillies, seeded and sliced finely
1 stalk spring onion, chopped
300 g flour
1¾ cups thick coconut milk, from 1 grated coconut
2 eggs
1 teaspoon salt
3 red chillies, seeded and sliced finely
1 stalk spring onion, chopped
reserved shallot crisps

Heat oil in a *kuali* and lightly brown shallots. Drain and leave aside for garnishing.

Season prawns with salt and pepper and leave for 15 minutes.

Put seasoned prawns in the *kuali* and stir fry for 2 minutes until cooked. Add red chillies and spring onion. Remove and cool.

Sift flour into a small mixing bowl. Stir in coconut milk a little at a time. Lightly beat eggs with a fork and mix into batter together with salt. Stir in cooled prawn mixture.

Grease and heat egg-shaped *kuih cara* moulds (p 127) over very low heat. Spoon 1 tablespoon prawn batter or enough to fill each individual mould and cook for 8-10 minutes.

When *kuih* is almost cooked, garnish with red chillies, spring onion and shallot crisps. Remove with a small butter knife when completely cooked.

Sri Kaya Perigi

Preparation: 30 minutes
Steaming: 40 minutes

1 medium pumpkin, approximately 3 kg and about 23-25½ cm in diameter
300 g palm sugar (gula melaka), chopped finely
¼ cup water
7 eggs
1¾ cups thick coconut milk, from 1½ grated coconuts
1 dessertspoon pandan juice

Wash pumpkin and carefully cut a 10-12½ cm circle from the top. Using a spoon, remove seed and soft portion to leave a hollow case. Skin top circle. Cut pumpkin (from scooped out portion and top circle) into neat 1¼ cm cubes. Place pumpkin cubes into pumpkin case.

Place chopped palm sugar and water in a small saucepan and cook over low heat, stirring until sugar dissolves. Strain.

In a mixing bowl, stir eggs lightly with coconut milk. Add pandan juice and palm sugar syrup. Mix well.

Strain egg mixture into pumpkin case. Stir mixture, then place pumpkin case in a large steamer. Steam for 35-40 minutes until pumpkin is cooked. Serve soft custard hot or cold in small bowls.

Kuih Bangkit

Prepration: 15 minutes
Baking: 25 minutes
Oven setting: 175 °C
Makes: 200

Kuih bangkit cutters

1 packet (500 g) tapioca flour
5 pandan leaves, washed, towelled dry and cut into 5 cm pieces
2 eggs
1 extra teaspoon egg yolk
180 g castor sugar
1 teaspoon vanilla essence
½ cup thick coconut milk, from ½ large grated white coconut

Pan-fry tapioca flour with pandan leaves over high heat for 10 minutes. Reduce heat and continue to stir fry for another 5 minutes. Remove and cool thoroughly.

Measure 480 g of the tapioca flour and keep remainder for flouring working board. Whisk the whole eggs and extra teaspoon of egg yolk, castor sugar, and vanilla essence until very light and fluffy. Sift in tapioca flour and mix with the hand until mixture resembles fine breadcrumbs. Add thick coconut milk a little at a time and knead into a firm pliable dough. Place on unfloured board and continue kneading for 5 minutes.

Roll out dough to a thickness of ³/₄ cm on a lightly floured board. Stamp with small *kuih bangkit* cutters. Place on baking tray floured with tapioca flour. Bake in moderate oven for 25 minutes. Cool before storing in air-tight containers.

Old love letter moulds, which are now difficult to find, have very intricate designs that turn out beautiful on the crunchy snack. Old wives swear that your 'love letters' are only as good as your charcoal fire but in these days of modern living, a gas stove is grudgingly accepted. Do not fret if the first few love letters do not turn out nicely as the moulds have to be well-seasoned during grilling.

Kuih Kapit (Love Letters)

A must for the Chinese New Year and *Hari Raya* – rolled or in quarters.

Preparation: 20 minutes
Baking: 1 hour
Makes: 100

120 g rice flour
30 g plain flour
150 g coarse or granulated sugar
2 cups coconut milk + ½ cup (for diluting batter),
from 1 grated coconut
2 eggs
3 egg yolks

Sift rice and plain flours into a mixing bowl. Put in sugar and slowly add coconut milk. Stir until smooth. Add whole eggs and egg yolks and whisk until blended. Strain mixture.

Lightly grease 2-3 love letter moulds with a piece of muslin cloth dipped in oil. Heat moulds over gas stove or charcoal fire. Place open mould over bowl of batter and pour a ladleful of batter into the mould. Close the mould tightly and bake over low gas flame or charcoal fire for approximately ½ minute on each side. When golden in colour, remove and immediately roll into fingers (p 88) or fold into a quarter (p 1). If folding into quarters, press lightly with tin cover to level surface. When the batter gets thick, dilute with 1-2 tablespoons of the reserved coconut milk.

Cool and store in an air-tight container.

Goreng Pisang

A simple snack that is very often found at teatime – even with the disappearance of the *goreng pisang* man who used to be found in almost every neighbourhood.

Two different batters are given here. Batter (2) gives a harder, crunchier crust and keeps crunchier longer with the addition of rice flour.

Preparation: 10 minutes
Frying: 5 minutes
Makes: 6

Batter (1)
45 g self-raising flour
½ cup water, approximate
oil for deep frying
6 small pisang raja, skinned

Sift self-raising flour into a bowl. Add salt and water. Mix to a smooth thick batter. Dip and coat bananas with the batter. Carefully drop into hot oil. Fry until golden brown. Drain on absorbent paper. Serve hot.

Batter (2)
A
45 g plain flour
30 g rice flour
⅓ teaspoon baking powder
¼ teaspoon salt, sifted
¾ cup water, approximate

Sift **A** and add water slowly. Mix into a smooth batter, making sure it is not too thick but just enough to coat the back of a spoon. Follow above method.

Sweet Potato Fritters
Skin and cut 1 medium size sweet potato into ¾ cm thick slices. Use either batter (1) or (2) and follow method.

Kuih Koci

For an alternative filling, try that used for *Nyonya Kueh Mah Chee* (p 44).

Preparation: 20 minutes
Cooking: 25 minutes
Steaming: 15 minutes
Makes: 20

2 tablespoons oil
90 g palm sugar (gula melaka), *chopped into small pieces*
150 g grated white coconut
¼ teaspoon salt
300 g glutinous rice flour
A
1¼ cup coconut milk, from 1 grated coconut
½ tablespoon sugar
¼ teaspoon salt
2 dessertspoons oil
20 pieces (15 cm square) banana leaves,
scalded, wiped dry and greased

Heat oil in a *kuali* and melt palm sugar over medium heat. Add grated coconut and salt and stir fry till evenly coated with palm syrup. Remove and cool.

Sift glutinous rice flour into a bowl. Mix in **A**. Knead to form a soft dough. Divide into 20 portions and form each into round balls. Flatten each round of dough with the hand and put in a teaspoonful of coconut filling in the centre. Gather and seal edges to enclose the filling.

Fold a piece of banana leaf into a cone and put in filled dough. Wrap and tuck in the ends. Staple securely with a stapler.

Arrange on a steamer and steam over rapidly boiling water for 15 minutes.

Abok-Abok Sago

A simple dessert that can be prepared very quickly for unexpected guests or for something different at tea. Use different colours and make a very attractive dish for parties.

Preparation: 15 minutes
Steaming: 1 hour
Makes: approximately 16 pieces

180 g pearl sago (p 112)
120 g grated white coconut
120 g granulated sugar
¼ teaspoon salt
4 teaspoons pandan juice (p 114)
(blend 5 cut-up pandan leaves with a little water)
2-3 drops green colouring

Put pearl sago in a strainer. Wash under a running tap to get rid of excess starch. Drain well.

Mix sago with grated coconut, sugar and salt in a mixing bowl. Divide into two portions. Combine pandan juice with green colouring and mix into one portion leaving the other uncoloured.

Grease a 16½cm square baking tin or dish. Spread the green-coloured portion on the base. Press down firmly. Steam over rapidly boiling water for 10-15 minutes. Pour the uncoloured portion over the green layer. Spread and press down firmly and steam for 45 minutes until sago is transparent.

Remove from steamer and cool thoroughly before cutting into squares or diamond-shapes.

Coconut Sago

An even simpler snack that does not require steaming. Make it in as many colours as you like. Coconut sago can also be served chilled.

Preparation: 15 minutes
Cooking: 20 minutes
Makes: approximately 12 pieces

boiling water
90 g pearl sago (p 112)
2 cups water
120 g sugar
2 pandan leaves, knotted
pinch of salt
a few drops red or yellow colouring
½ grated white coconut mixed with a pinch of salt

Pour boiling water onto sago and leave for 30 seconds. Pour scalded sago into a strainer. Wash under a running tap to get rid of excess starch. Drain well.

Put water, sugar, pandan leaves and salt in a saucepan. Stir over low heat until sugar dissolves. Bring to a boil, remove pandan leaves and add sago. Continue to cook over low heat by stirring until sago turns transparent. Stir in red or yellow colouring.

Pour sago into a pan or dish 15 cm x 10 cm lightly greased with butter. Spread and level surface. Cool thoroughly before cutting into squares. Roll each piece in grated coconut.

Kuih Talam

Another two-layered sweet snack that looks difficult but is in fact easy to make.

Preparation: 15 minutes
Cooking: 5 minutes
Steaming: 35 minutes
Makes: approximately 16

240 g rice flour
120 g tapioca flour
300 g palm sugar (gula melaka), *chopped*
2 cups water
120 g rice flour
180 g castor sugar
2 cups coconut milk, from 1 grated white coconut
½ teaspoon salt

Sift rice and tapioca flours into mixing bowl. Put palm sugar and water in a saucepan and bring to a slow boil stirring until sugar dissolves. Pour into the flour mixture and mix with a wooden spoon. Pour batter into a 22 cm cake pan and steam over rapidly boiling water for 15 minutes.

Sift remaining 120 g rice flour into a mixing bowl. Add sugar, coconut milk and salt and mix well. Cook over low heat for 5 minutes until sugar dissolves. Pour warm mixture over palm sugar layer and steam for 20 minutes over medium heat.

Banana Coconut Cream with Palm Syrup

Preparation: 10 minutes
Cooking: 15 minutes

1 packet (85 g) green bean flour (hoen kwe)
3 cups coconut milk, from 1 grated white coconut
½ teaspoon vanilla essence
¼ teaspoon banana essence
90 g sugar
3 tablespoons evaporated milk
3 green bananas, sliced

A
240 g palm sugar (gula melaka), *chopped*
30 g granulated sugar
1 cup water
2 pandan leaves, knotted

Blend green bean flour with a little coconut milk until smooth. Add remaining coconut milk, vanilla essence, banana essence and sugar. Cook over low heat, stirring all the time with a wooden spoon.

When mixture is hot, stir in evaporated milk and continue stirring until mixture boils and thickens. Remove from heat and stir in banana slices. Pour into a 17 cm x 27 cm tray. Allow to cool then chill in the refrigerator.

Place **A** in a saucepan and boil over low heat until sugar has dissolved. Strain.

Stamp chilled banana coconut cream into rounds with a pastry cutter or cut into squares. Serve in individual serving dishes topped with a little palm syrup.

Sambal Ikan

This will keep well in an air-tight container in the refrigerator for as long as 4-6 weeks. It goes well with rice and porridge and is delicious as a sandwich spread.

Preparation: 20 minutes
Cooking: about 1 hour

1 kg horse mackerel (*ikan kembong*)
1½ cups thick coconut milk, from 1½ grated coconuts

A
15 red chillies
4 cm ginger
4 stalks lemon grass
15 shallots
3 cloves garlic
4 pieces dried tamarind skin (p 107)
2 teaspoons salt
2 teaspoons sugar

Grind **A**. Steam fish for 12 minutes or until cooked. When cool, remove bones and lightly mash fish with the back of a spoon.

Combine coconut milk with **A** and mashed fish and bring to a slow boil over moderate heat. Boil for 5 minutes stirring frequently, then lower heat and fry continuously for approximately 50 minutes, taking care mixture does not stick to pan, until completely dry.

Glutinous Rice Sandwich

This recipe uses *sambal ikan* but you can try it with *sambal udang* (p 5) or any leftover minced meat curry. The coconut milk used in this recipe must be thick and from the first 'squeeze'. It should come to just above the level of rice.

Preparation: 15 minutes
Cooking: 10 minutes
Steaming: 30 minutes
Makes: approximately 36 pieces

600 g glutinous rice, soaked for 2 hours
1 ½ teaspoons salt
enough coconut milk to cover rice, from 1 grated coconut
8 tablespoons sambal ikan

Drain water from glutinous rice and place in container. Add salt and enough coconut milk to cover rice. Stir well. Steam over rapidly boiling water for 30 minutes.

Line a 21-22 cm square cake tin with banana leaves, so that the ends are slightly higher than the rims. Spoon one third of rice into tin and press down firmly and evenly with the back of a spoon. Sprinkle half of the *sambal ikan* evenly over surface. Spoon half of the remaining cooked glutinous rice to cover *sambal*. Press down again with back of spoon and repeat process with remaining *sambal ikan* and glutinous rice. Cover with a piece of banana leaf and place a heavy object on surface to pack rice firmly. Leave to cool thoroughly before cutting.

Lempar Udang

A savoury teatime snack that is also good for cocktail parties or buffets. This has a natural sweetness of fresh prawns. A variation using dried prawns is also given. Serve both and surprise your guests.

Preparation: 1 hour
Cooking: 45 minutes
Grilling: 15 minutes
Grill setting: 175°C
Makes: 16

A
5 shallots
1 clove garlic
1 candlenut
1 red chilli
1 dessertspoon coriander powder (p 43)
300 g glutinous rice, washed and drained
2 cups coconut milk, from ½ grated coconut
1 teaspoon salt
2 teaspoons sugar
1 tablespoon oil
300 g shelled prawns, chopped
12 g grated white coconut, roasted and ground
1 ½ teaspoons sugar
¾ teaspoon salt
16 pieces (12½ cm x 10 cm) banana leaves, scalded and wiped dry

Grind **A**.

In a heatproof dish, combine glutinous rice, coconut milk, salt and sugar. Steam over rapidly boiling water for 25 minutes. Remove from steamer.

Heat oil in a *kuali* and fry **A** for 1-2 minutes until fragrant. Put in prawns and stir fry till cooked. Add roasted coconut, sugar and salt.

Place a tablespoonful of glutinous rice and spread in the centre of a banana leaf. Put 2 teaspoonfuls of filling on it. Top with another tablespoonful of rice. Roll up into a neat roll and secure ends with sharpened cocktail sticks. Brush rolls with a little cooking oil.

Grill over charcoal fire or electric grill for 15 minutes turning the rolls occasionally.

Lempar Udang with Dried Prawns

This has a nice aroma of fragrant dried prawns.

Makes: 15

A
120 g peeled shallots
1 red chilli, sliced and finely ground
60 g dried prawns, soaked
2 teaspoonfuls roasted coriander powder
120 g white grated coconut, pan-fried for 3-5 minutes
3½ teaspoons sugar
¼ teaspoon salt
15 pieces banana leaves, (14 cm X 12½ cm) scalded and wiped dry

Heat oil and fry **A** for 5 minutes or until fragrant. Add coriander powder, roasted coconut, sugar and salt and fry for a further 5 minutes. Remove and cool.

Use filling as for *Lempar Udang*.

Ayam Pulut Panggang

Two recipes here, the second actually a Nonya prepration.

(1)

This is curry-flavoured. With coconut milk added, it is moist and does not keep well.

Preparation: 1 hour
Cooking: 40 minutes
Grilling: 15 minutes
Oven setting: 175°C
Makes: 12

300 g glutinous rice, washed and drained
2 cups coconut milk, from ½ grated coconut
(reserve 2 tablespoons extra milk for filling)
1 teaspoon salt
3 pandan leaves, knotted
300 g chicken, finely diced
¾ teaspoon salt
1 tablespoon oil
A
6 shallots and 2 cloves garlic, ground
2 tablespoons curry powder mixed into a paste with 2 tablespoons water
2 tablespoons reserved coconut milk
12 pieces (15 cm x 12 cm) banana leaves, scalded and wiped dry

In a heatproof dish, combine glutinous rice, coconut milk and salt. Put in pandan leaves. Steam over rapidly boiling water for 25 minutes.

Season chicken with salt for 15 minutes.

Heat oil and fry **A** until fragrant. Add curry powder paste and chicken and fry for a few minutes. Put in coconut milk and cook until gravy is dry.

Remove rice from steamer. Take a tablespoonful of glutinous rice and spread it in the centre of a banana leaf. Put a dessertspoonful of chicken filling on it. Top with another tablespoon of rice. Roll up into a firm roll and secure both ends with sharpened cocktail sticks or use a stapler to staple the ends. Brush rolls with a little cooking oil. Roast the rolls over slow charcoal fire or grill in an electric grill for 15 minutes turning the rolls from one side to the other.

(2)

This recipe, using only coriander powder and without coconut milk, is a typical Nonya preparation with the fragrant aroma of coriander permeating every bite.

Preparation: 1 hour
Cooking: 40 minutes
Grilling: 15 minutes
Oven setting: 175°C
Makes: 12

400 g glutinous rice, washed, soaked for 1 hour and drained
½ teaspoon salt
4 tablespoons oil
150 g peeled shallots, sliced
3 cloves garlic, chopped

A
150 g chicken, finely diced
2 teaspoons coriander powder (p 43), roasted
2 teaspoons sugar
½ teaspoon salt
½ teaspoon pepper
¼ teaspoon dark soya sauce

12 pieces (15 cm x 12½ cm) banana leaves, scalded and wiped dry

Put rice in a heatproof dish with salt and water to just below the level of rice. Steam over rapidly boiling water for 30 minutes. Leave aside.

Heat oil in a *kuali* and brown shallots and garlic. Drain and remove from oil. Pour off excess oil leaving 2 tablespoons in *kuali*. Put in fried shallots and garlic again together with **A**. Fry until fragrant and cook for approximately 5 minutes. Drain off excess oil and cool.

Follow method as for the first recipe.

INDIAN FARE

Indian breads and curries:
(clockwise on griddle) *Chapati* (p 152), *Chapati* with Spicy Potato Filling (p 153) and Blackgram *Thosai* (p 157); (anti-clockwise from left) *Appam* (p 160), *Paratha* (p 150), *Puttu* (p 159), *Naan* (p 154), *Rava Thosai* (p 158), Onion Sambal (p 177), Coconut Sambal (p 176), Brinjal Puree (p 169), Yoghurt (p 170), Dhal Curry (p 175), Potato and Pea Curry (p 171) and Sardine and Brinjal Curry (p 167).

Paratha

Paratha

Paratha – *roti paratha* or *roti canai* as it is known in Singapore and Malaysia – is a flat pancake-like bread indigenous to India. Circular or rectangular in shape, it is a hot favourite, especially for breakfast, with almost all who have lived in this part of the world. Not only are they sustaining, they are also cheap and easily available from hawker stalls, coffee shops and restaurants.

Paratha is basically bread made from flour, eggs, sugar and salt, kneaded into a stiff dough with water and margarine, butter or ghee. It contains no leavening agent at all as heat alone is enough to raise the thinly flattened dough. The moisture in the dough is converted to steam and creates an expanding pocket that puffs up the light and soft paper thin dough. A well-made *paratha* is crisp outside and soft inside. Kneading the dough well is important as this incorporates air into the dough and makes it light.

The most difficult part in *paratha* making is whirling and flipping the dough into a paper-thin sheet. It is an art and the *paratha*-man makes a great show of it. It takes practice (with a towel first) till you get the hang of it. If like mè, the magic of the flip escapes you, don't panic. You can still make excellent *paratha* simply by carefully stretching the dough. It takes double the time, but the end result is nothing short of perfect. But do be careful with long fingernails which are disastrous when attempting this procedure.

Paratha is usually served with curries to help 'mop' up the gravy and sometimes with a sprinkling of sugar.

Preparation: 30 minutes
Cooking: 1 hour
Makes: 14

1 kg plain flour
3 ½ teaspoons salt
90 g sugar
60 g ghee, butter or margarine
1 cup water
1 cup milk
1 egg, lightly beaten
oil or ghee for greasing and cooking

Sift flour into a mixing bowl, add salt and sugar. Blend fat into flour with a pastry cutter.

Make a well in the centre and pour in water, milk and egg mixture. Knead with hands for 10-15 minutes into a firm smooth dough or beat in an electric mixer for 5-7 minutes using the dough hook.

Divide dough into 14 equal portions. Roll into round balls and rub oil generously over surface of each ball. Place in an air-tight well-greased plastic container and leave overnight.

Grease a smooth working surface. With oiled hands flatten a piece of dough into a 20 cm circle. Carefully lift and stretch dough into a paper thin rectangle. Sprinkle a little oil on surface of stretched dough and fold into thirds by bringing one third over to the middle, then folding the remaining third over it. Repeat folding with the other two ends, forming a square. If you prefer round *roti paratha* stretch or flip dough into a thin rectangle, fold in the two longest sides then lift dough at one end like a rope and curl into a round bun. Leave aside on greased surface to rest for 15 minutes. Flatten by lightly pressing with the fingers into a thick 20 cm round.

Sprinkle oil or ghee generously on flat griddle. Place *paratha* on hot griddle and cook over low heat, turning *paratha* and spreading more oil or ghee until they are golden brown. Remove from griddle and place on a plate. To loosen the layers and keep *paratha* fluffy, squash the *paratha* with both hands whilst still hot. Serve hot with *dhal*, mutton or fish curries.

Murtabak

Variation of the *roti paratha* that gives you an Indian pizza.

Preparation: 1 hour
Cooking: 1 hour
Makes: 4-5 *murtabak*s

500 g minced mutton, beef or chicken
3 tablespoons curry powder for meat
1 teaspoon salt
4 tablespoons oil
2 onions, coarsely chopped
1/2 recipe of paratha *dough*
3 onions, halved and sliced
4 green chillies, thinly sliced
4-5 eggs

Season meat with curry powder and salt and leave aside for 15 minutes. Heat oil and lightly brown onions. Add seasoned meat and stir fry for 10 minutes or until cooked. Remove and cool. (This filling is sufficient for 4-5 *murtabak*s.)

Prepare dough as for *paratha* recipe. Stretch or flip dough into a paper thin sheet. Break an egg in the centre of rectangular sheet of dough and carefully spread egg over the middle portion. Sprinkle a little onion and green chillies over the egg and then one fifth of the minced meat filling. Fold in the four sides like an envelope into a neat square.

Carefully and quickly lift *murtabak* using both hands onto well greased hot griddle. Fry *murtabak* on both sides until golden brown in colour and cooked through.

Serve hot with cut cucumbers and onions topped with tomato sauce.

Paratha also has interesting variations. If you add an egg, and if you like, chopped onions, it becomes an egg *paratha*. If you add minced meat, it becomes a *murtabak*.

Chapati (Unleavened Bread)

Chapati is part of the daily diet for Northern Indians and when made with margarine can be a healthy alternative to rice. The dough for *chapati*, like all Indian breads, must be properly kneaded for a light-textured result.

Here are two recipes, one plain and the other with potato stuffing for special occasions.

Preparation: 30 minutes
Cooking: 15 minutes
Makes: 6 *chapati*

150 g wholemeal (atta) *flour*
½ teaspoon salt
½ tablespoon ghee, margarine or oil
½ cup lukewarm water

Wholemeal/*atta* flour
This is a finely-milled wheat flour that is used for *chapati* and other Indian breads. It's available from Indian provision stores and even supermarkets.

Put wholemeal flour in a mixing bowl and add salt. Rub in ghee, margarine or oil. Add water a little at a time and mix to a firm soft dough. Lightly flour the board with wholemeal flour and knead dough for at least 10 minutes. The longer the dough is kneaded the lighter will be the *chapati*. Put dough in a plastic bag or wrap with a damp tea towel and let it stand for 3 hours, preferably overnight for even lighter *chapati*.

Divide and shape the dough into six round balls. Roll out on lightly floured board into flat circular shapes, the size of a saucer.

Heat a heavy frying pan or griddle until very hot. Place a *chapati* on it and cook for 1 minute on each side, pressing lightly around the edges with a folded tea towel. Bubbles will appear on the surface and when cooked the *chapati* will have brown spots. Cover the *chapati* with a dry tea towel until ready to be served.

Serve with your favourite vegetable or meat curries and cut cucumbers and onions mixed with lime juice.

Chapati With Spicy Potato Filling

Preparation: 1 hour
Cooking: 1 hour
Makes: 16 stuffed *chapatis*

1 tablespoon oil
2 onions, finely chopped
1 dessertspoon ground chillies (p 94)
2 potatoes, mashed
1 medium size carrot, grated
1 teaspoon salt
1 stalk spring onion, chopped
1 sprig coriander leaves (p 43), chopped
500 g wholemeal (atta) flour (p 152)
1½ cups water
½ teaspoon salt
3 tablespoons ghee

Heat oil and lightly brown onions. Add chillies, mashed potatoes, grated carrot, salt and chopped spring onion and coriander leaves. Mix well. Remove from heat and allow to cool.

Put wholemeal flour into a mixing bowl with salt. Mix into a firm ball of dough by adding water a little at a time. Spread 1 tablespoon of ghee on the dough and continue kneading. Repeat with another tablespoon of ghee. Lastly spread the last tablespoon of ghee onto the lump of dough and allow to stand for 30 minutes.

Divide into small balls of dough. Flatten dough with the palm of your hands. Dip both sides into a little flour. Place *chapati* on a wooden board and roll out with a rolling pin.

Brush with a little ghee and spread 1 tablespoon of spicy potato filling evenly on surface. Fold into half and then fold again to seal filling. Dip again into flour and roll out again into a thin square of *chapati*.

Place *chapati* onto a flat pan over medium heat and brown both sides. Brush *chapati* with ghee on both sides while frying.

Serve with plain yoghurt (p 170) or with Mixed Vegetable Curry (p 172).

Naan (Punjabi Leavened Bread)

Naan, which can be found in all Northern Indian restaurants around the world, are traditionally baked in clay ovens called *tandoori* (from where one gets *tandoori* chicken). But the simplified method used in this recipe will produce just as good results.

Preparation: 30 minutes
Baking: 15 minutes
Oven temperature: 200°C
Makes: 10

1 teaspoon sugar
¾ cup warm water
30 g compressed yeast
420 g plain flour
2 teaspoons salt
2 teaspoons sugar
45 g butter, at room temperature
¼ cup yoghurt (p 170)
1 egg, lightly beaten
a little melted ghee
black cummin seeds

Dissolve sugar in water and drop in yeast. Allow to stand 10-15 minutes until mixture turns frothy.

Sift flour into a bowl. Add salt and sugar and blend in butter with a pastry blender. Pour yoghurt and egg mixture together with frothy yeast mixture into the flour. Beat in electric mixer for 3-5 minutes until dough is smooth and elastic. Cover with a damp towel and leave to rise until mixture doubles in bulk, which takes approximately 1 hour.

Preheat the oven to hot. Place 3 ungreased trays into the oven to preheat.

Turn the dough out, knead lightly and divide into 10 pieces. Roll into balls and roll each on a lightly floured board into a thick circle of dough about 1½ cm in thickness. Stretch one end of dough to form a teardrop shape. Brush with melted ghee and sprinkle with black cummin seeds.

Bake for 12-15 minutes until puffy and golden. Serve with Special Chicken Curry (p 166), *Korma* (p 164) or *tandoori* chicken.

Puri

A light puffed-up bread, *puri* are almost identical to *chapati*, except that they are deep fried in hot oil. Serve it for high tea, lunch or for a light dinner.

Preparation: 30 minutes
Cooking: 30 minutes
Makes: 24

A
240 g wholemeal (atta) flour (p 152)
120 g plain flour
60 g semolina
1 teaspoon salt
2 dessertspoons cornoil
water
oil for deep frying

Sift **A** into a bowl, add salt and cornoil. Knead into a firm dough with a little water. Form into small balls and flatten into thin rounds with a roller on a floured board.

Deep fry in hot oil in a *kuali* till *puri* are puffed up and light brown (the secret is to spoon oil over top of *puri* while the bottom is being fried.) Serve hot with *Kabuli* (p 174) or any favourite curry.

Potato Puri

These are *puris* made from potatoes and not stuffed like the *chapati* recipe. Deliciously light, they will puff up in a spectacular fashion – great for dinner parties.

Preparation: 30 minutes
Cooking: 10 minutes
Makes: 10

125 g potatoes, peeled
120 g plain flour
³/₄ teaspoon salt
2 tablespoons lukewarm water
oil for deep frying

Boil potatoes until very soft and finely mash with a potato masher or fork. Mix the cool mashed potato with the flour and salt. Add water and knead well to make a firm soft dough. Knead for at least 10 minutes or until dough is smooth. Cover and leave to stand for 1 hour.

Divide into 10 equal portions and form into round balls. Roll out on a lightly floured board into thin flat circular shapes.

Deep fry on both sides until golden in colour. *Puri* will puff up like a balloon. Drain on absorbent paper and serve immediately with vegetable or meat curries.

Thosai

This is a Southern Indian shallow fried pancake which is thin and slightly sour (the sourish elusive tang comes from the blackgram or *ulundu*). It's eaten at breakfast, lunch, dinner or just about anytime.

These three recipes will keep *thosai* lovers happy for a long time. Only the ingredients and preparation differ but the method for cooking remains the same. If you don't have the correct griddle, use a non-stick frying pan. Heat and grease the base with very little ghee or oil. Pour in a ladle of batter and swirl pan around to make a thin circular pancake. Cook until the underside is slightly brown and the edges leave the sides of pan. Turn and cook the other side. However, this method does not produce the ever-popular paper *thosai*. Serve *thosai* with coconut sambal or any other dry vegetable curry.

And if you're wondering why cooked rice is used, this just helps to ferment the *thosai* mixture.

Preparation: 10 minutes
Cooking: 15 minutes
Makes: 9

50 g blackgram with skin (p 157)
180 g uncooked rice
60 g cooked rice
¼ teaspoon fenugreek
1½ cups water
1 teaspoon salt
¼ turmeric powder
cooking or sesame (gingerly *oil*/minyak bijan*) oil or ghee*

This first recipe has a delicate taste of fenugreek and is light yellow in colour. Fenugreek (*halba*) gives a tangy bitter-sweet flavour to the otherwise plain thosais.

Soak blackgram, uncooked rice and fenugreek for 6 hours. Drain, removing skin of blackgram, and put into a blender with the cooked rice and water. Add salt and turmeric powder and grind to a smooth batter. Leave to ferment for 8-9 hours, preferably overnight.

Grease a hot griddle over low heat with cooking or sesame oil or ghee. Using a ladle, pour a ladle of batter on centre of the griddle. Spread the batter immediately with the back of ladle on centre of the griddle. Immediately spread batter with the back of ladle in a clockwise motion to make a thin pancake with circular ripples.

Cover griddle (a rice cooker cover will do nicely) and cook for about ½ a minute until the underside turns slightly brown. Remove from griddle with the help of a flat fish slice or spatula. Repeat till the batter is used up making sure the griddle is greased each time.

Skinned and unskinned blackgram (*ulundu*), used for *thosai*, *vadai* (p 185) and even as a seasoning by Southern Indians for vegetable dishes.

(2) *Blackgram Thosai*

My favourite – white in colour and just as soft and springy as the first recipe.

Two cups of *Mahsuri* rice can be used instead of a combination of *Mahsuri* and parboiled rice. However, if parboiled rice (or Indian rice as it is sometimes known) is used, the mixture takes a shorter time to ferment and the *thosai* will taste more sourish. Blend the mixture at 15 minute intervals to ensure that the rice is not grainy but blended smooth and fine, and the blender will also not burn out this way.

Preparation: 30 minutes
Cooking: 30 minutes
Makes: 25-30

300 g Mahsuri *rice B2, washed and soaked for 6 hours*
300 g *parboiled rice, washed and soaked for 6 hours*
240 g *blackgram, washed and soaked for 6 hours*
2 *teaspoons salt*
2 *tablespoons cooked rice*
2 *cups water, approximate*
cooking or sesame oil (gingerly oil/minyak bijan) *or ghee for greasing*

Drain *Mahsuri* and parboiled rice and place in blender.

Rub the soaked blackgram in between palms to remove the husk. Do this several times then wash away the husks and drain well. Add the blackgram, salt and cooked rice and blend the mixture into a very fine batter, adding enough water to obtain a pouring consistency.

Pour batter into a bowl and leave covered for 8-9 hours, or overnight, to rise.

Follow method for cooking as for the first recipe.

(3) Rava (Semolina) Thosai

A grainy textured thosai with a good 'bite'.

Preparation: 30 minutes
Cooking: 30 minutes
Makes: 10

120 g semolina
120 g wheat flour
120 g rice flour
1 tablespoon cooked rice
1 onion
1 green chilli
1 small sprig curry leaves, remove the stem
½ tablespoon salt
2¼ cups water

Blend all the ingredients until fine in an electric blender. Leave overnight. Follow method for cooking as for the first recipe.

Idiyapum (Puttumayam/String-Hopper)

Great at breakfast with brown sugar and grated coconut or with curries and *sothi* for lunch or dinner. You can also fry left-overs with egg and onions for breakfast or a snack.

Preparation: 15 minutes
Steaming: 10 minutes
Makes: 14

480 g rice flour
½ teaspoon salt
2 ½ cups hot boiling water
1 teaspoon sugar
ghee

Sift rice flour into a large bowl and stir in salt. Add boiling hot water and mix into a stiff paste with a wooden spoon. Sprinkle in sugar and stir to mix well. Dough should be light and not sticky to the touch.

Lightly grease two steamer trays with a little ghee. Fill string-hopper mould (p 180) with dough and press mould with a circular motion to form a lacy circle the size of a small saucer (approximately 10 cm in diameter).

Make several circles of string-hoppers to fill tray, taking care not to overlap. Steam over rapidly boiling water for 10 minutes and serve with *Sothi* (p 173) and your favourite curries.

Sting-hopper mould

Puttu

Puttu is a Ceylonese dish usually served for dinner with hot sambals and curries. It is also popular for breakfast and can be served with sweet accompaniments such as lightly mashed bananas (*pisang rastali*) topped with brown or white sugar or with coconut and grated palm sugar.

Preparation: 30 minutes
Steaming: 10 minutes
Serves: 4-5 persons

360 g rice flour
½ teaspoon salt
1 cup hot boiling water
60 g grated coconut
1 dessertspoon rice flour
1 teaspoonful sugar

Puttu should be steamed in a bamboo cylinder. This is time consuming but worth trying as it gives a special fragrance. The bamboo cylinder is filled with alternating layers of *puttu* mixture and grated coconut, then pressed down gently and steamed. The method used in this recipe however, is an improvised time-saving one. To ensure that *puttu* turn out soft, the water has to be at boiling point and added immediately to the flour. This partly helps to cook the dough.

Sift rice flour into a large bowl. Stir in salt. Add hot water and mix with a wooden spoon, then rub gently with the fingertips to combine mixture into a stiff crumbly dough.

Place a piece of tracing paper on working board. Turn dough onto the paper. Sprinkle a dessertspoon of rice flour over dough. Cut mixture with a pastry or biscuit cutter into pea-size crumbs. Sprinkle with sugar and mix gently with the fingertips. Line a steamer tray with a piece of dampened muslin cloth over the mixture.

Steam over rapidly boiling water for 10 minutes. Serve *puttu* with fish, Chicken or Mutton curry (p 166).

Appam (Hopper)

Rice flour pancakes that make a nice and unusual breakfast dish. Leave out the cream and serve *appam* for lunch or dinner with your favourite curries.

Preparation: 20 minutes
Cooking: 1 hour
Makes: 16

360 g rice
2 tablespoons cooked rice
2 tablespoons plain flour
2 tablespoons sugar
½ teaspoon salt
1 cup thick coconut milk and 1½ cups thin coconut milk, from 1 large grated coconut
1 dessertspoon baking powder
brown sugar

Wash and soak rice for 5 hours. Strain. Put strained rice, cooked rice, flour, sugar, salt and ¾ cup of the thin coconut milk into a liquidiser and blend to a fine paste. Pour into a pot and add remaining thin coconut milk. Leave to ferment for 12 hours, preferably overnight. Refrigerate the thick coconut milk.

The next day, add baking powder into fermented mixture and stir well. Heat and lightly grease a small *kuali* and pour two tablespoons of batter into the centre. Swivel the *kuali* to spread batter into a thin pancake. The centre of the pancake should be thick. Quickly add 1 tablespoon of the thick coconut milk. Cover the *kuali* and let it cook over low heat until sides of *appam* are lightly brown.

Remove and serve sprinkled with a little brown sugar or with Coconut *Sambal* (p 176).

Chicken Beriani

A one-pot meal that's great for special occassions. Just serve with curries, a fresh salad and *pappadum*.

Preparation: 30 minutes
Cooking: 50 minutes
Serves: 3

2 *whole chicken thighs and 2 chicken wings, cleaned and left whole*
1 *teaspoon salt*
2 *tablespoons ghee*
1 *tablespoon butter*
2 *large onions, sliced*

A

2 *cm piece cinnamon*
2 *cloves*
3 *cardamons, remove skin*
¾ *tablespoon cummin seeds*
½ *tablespoon fennel seeds*
¼ *teaspoon pepper*
2 *cm ginger*
4 *cloves garlic*
¼ *piece of a nutmeg*

2 *tomatoes, quartered*
2 *sprigs coriander leaves (p 43), finely chopped*
2 *sprigs mint, finely chopped*
¾ *cup water*
10 *cashew nuts, ground and combined with ¼ cup evaporated milk*

B

300 *g* Basmati *rice, washed and drained*
1 ½ *teaspoons salt*
½ *teaspoon rose essence*
few saffron strands, soaked in ½ cup boiling water
for 15 minutes and strained
3 *pandan leaves, tied into a knot*

60 *g raisins, fried*
shallot crisps
garlic crisps
12 *toasted cashew nuts*
cucumber slices

Basmati rice
Literally meaning 'flavoured' rice, this is a special long grain fragrant Indian rice which is more expensive that 'first grade' long grain rice. It gives the *beriani* a special fragrance and is almost synonymous with the dish. However, if it's not available, substitute with *Patna* rice.

Saffron
The most expensive spice in the world. It is the dried stigmas of the flowers of the saffron corcus. The fine orange-red threads about 4 cm long impart a bitter-honeylike taste and a strong yellow colour to food. Don't use turmeric as a substitute as it is altogether a different spice.

(cont'd on p 162)

Grind **A**. Season chicken with salt for 15 minutes.

Heat butter and ghee in a cooking pot and lightly brown onion. Dish out and leave aside. In the same ghee, fry **A** for a few minutes. Add tomatoes, fried onions, chopped coriander and mint leaves.

Put in chicken and stir fry. Add ¾ cup water and simmer until chicken is three-quarter cooked. Stir in milk and cashew nut mixture and simmer until chicken is cooked and gravy is thick. Add salt to taste.

In an electric rice cooker, put in **B**. Add enough water to come just a little above the rice. When rice is three-quarter cooked, add chicken gravy. Stir well to combine rice mixture. Put in chicken pieces and raisins and allow rice to cook through.

Just before serving, sprinkle with shallot and garlic crisps and toasted cashew nuts and decorate with cucumber slices.

Indian Rojak

Preparation: 1 hour
Cooking: 30 minutes
Serves: 6

Prawn Fritters
A
60 g self-raising flour, sifted
½ tablespoon turmeric powder
pinch of bicarbonate of soda
¼ teaspoon pepper
½ teaspoon sugar
pinch of salt
1 egg, beaten combined with 2 tablespoons water
2 shallots, finely chopped
30 g shelled chopped prawn

Put **A** into a mixing bowl. Make a smooth batter with egg and water mixture. Stir in shallots and prawns.

(cont'd on p 164)

Sauce Ingredients

3 tablespoons oil
1 dessertspoon ground dried chilles (*cili giling*), 20 shallots, and 1.5 cm turmeric root, ground
1 clove garlic
2 dessertspoons tamarind paste mixed with 2½-3 cups water or fresh prawn shell stock, if available, strained
180 g sweet potatoes, peeled, steamed and mashed
120 g sugar
1½ teaspoons salt
120 g roasted peanuts, finely ground
1 dessertspoon roasted sesame seeds

Heat oil in a *kuali* and fry ground ingredients until fragrant. Pour in tamarind water and stir in sweet potatoes, sugar and salt. When mixture comes to a boil, add roasted peanuts and lastly sesame seeds.

Salads Asian-style: (from top)
Indian *Rojak* with gravy (p 162),
Chinese *Rojak* with gravy (p 20)
and *Rojak Suun* (p 95).

Heat oil in a *kuali* for deep frying until hot. Reduce heat to medium and drop tablespoonful of batter into hot oil. Deep fry until golden brown in colour. Remove with a perforated ladle and drain on absorbent paper.

Fried Spicy Cuttlefish
½ a medium-size soaked cuttlefish (sotong kembang), cut into 1 cm pieces
2 tablespoons oil
1 teaspoon ground dried chilli (cili giling)
2 shallots, ground
A
¼ teaspoon salt
½ teaspoon sugar
2 tablespoons water

Wash cuttlefish and drain well.

Heat oil in a kuali and fry ground chilli and shallots until fragrant. Add cuttlefish and **A**. Stir fry over medium heat until cooked.

250 g beansprouts, tailed
½ cucumber, shredded
250 g turnip (bangkwang), skinned and shredded
3 pieces beancurd (taukwa), fried and sliced
2 potatoes, boiled, skinned, cut into wedges and deep fried
2 hardboiled eggs, quartered
prawn fritters, cut into wedges
fried spicy soaked cuttlefish, cut into 1 cm pieces

To serve, put a little of each of the ingredients in individual serving dishes and top with as much sauce as desired.

Chicken Korma

The more health-conscious may choose to substitute the coconut milk with water. This, however will loose the subtle fragrance of curry with coconut milk.

Preparation: 30 minutes
Cooking: 30 minutes

1 kg chicken, cut into serving size pieces
1 teaspoon salt
½ cup cooking oil

A
5 cm piece cinnamon
3 cloves
4 cardamons
2 onions, sliced

B
2.5 cm ginger
6 cloves garlic
4 green chillies
12 shallots
10 almonds or cashew nuts

C
1 tablespoon coriander powder (p 43)
¾ tablespoon cummin
½ tablespoon fennel
1 teaspoon pepper
1 teaspoon turmeric powder

1½ teaspoons salt
½ teaspoon sugar
3 cups thin coconut milk, from ½ grated coconut, or water
2 tomatoes, halved
2-3 green chillies, whole

shallot crisps
2-3 sprigs coriander leaves (p 43)

Season chicken with salt and leave for 30 minutes.

Heat oil in a deep cooking pot and fry **A** until onions are transparent. Add **B** and fry for 2-3 minutes and then add **C**. Put in chicken, salt and sugar and fry until well-coated with spices. Pour in coconut milk or water and simmer until chicken is tender. Add tomatoes and green chillies and simmer for 5 minutes.

Just before serving, garnish with shallot crisps and coriander leaves. Serve with String Hoppers (p 158) or *Paratha* (p 150).

Mutton Curry

In this curry, the strong mutton smell is 'masked' by a good combination of spices and the flavour of the spices pervades the curry, making it very aromatic. Surprise guests who don't normally like mutton. This is excellent served with rice or *Paratha* (p 150).

Preparation: 30 minutes
Cooking: 1 hour

1½ kg mutton, cut into 3 cm cubes
2.5 cm ginger, ground
2 cloves garlic, ground
1 tablespoon ghee
5 cm piece cinnamon stick
1 green chilli
4 cloves
16-18 shallots
5 cardamons
2 potatoes, cut into wedges lengthwise
1½ cups thick coconut milk and 5 cups thin coconut milk, from 1½ grated coconuts
½ teaspoon salt
2 teaspoons salt
35 g meat curry powder
juice of ½ a large lime

Follow method as for Special Chicken Curry. The only difference is the spices used and the omission of turmeric powder.

Indian or Bombay onions are rounder, dark purplish in colour and are less pungent.

Special Chicken Curry

This is my favourite chicken curry from the bewildering variety of Ceylonese curries. Although it's spiced, there is no suggestion of over-spicing in taste. It is well-laden with a tasty gravy but the goodness of the chicken is not lost. There is also a subtle aromatic hint of lime juice. It makes a delicious dish when served with string hoppers to sop up the gravy.

All cooks express their individuality through the use of spices. The delightful cook who taught me her specialities is an agile lady in her sixties. Her epicurean flair and remarkable ability to judge spicing with an eye for its colour, aroma and flavour is truly amazing.

Preparation: 30 minutes
Cooking: 40 minutes

2 kg chicken, cut into serving size pieces
2.5 cm ginger, ground
2 cloves garlic, ground
1 tablespoon ghee
7½ cm piece cinnamon stick
3 cloves
2 whole star anise
16-18 shallots (preferably Indian variety), sliced
1 green chilli
3 cardamons, remove pods
2 potatoes, cut into wedges lengthwise
1½ cups thick coconut milk and 5 cups thin coconut milk, from 1½ grated coconuts
½ teaspoon salt
1½ teaspoons turmeric powder
2 teaspoons salt
35 g meat curry powder
juice of ½ a large lime

Marinate chicken with ground ginger and garlic for 15 minutes. Heat *kuali* with ghee and stir fry cinnamon, cloves and star anise for 10 seconds or until fragrant.

Add shallots, green chilli and cardamon seeds, then the potatoes and fry till aromatic. Add chicken and stir fry for 2 minutes. Cover *kuali* and allow chicken to cook in its own juices until all the water evaporates. Turn chicken occasionally to prevent it from sticking to pan. Pour in thin coconut milk and cook covered for 15 minutes over medium heat.

Add thick coconut milk and when it comes to the boil, stir in turmeric powder and salt, and then curry powder. Cook for a further 15-20 minutes until chicken is tender. Lastly, add lime juice.

Sardine and Brinjal Curry

This is a curry that one can easily prepare for unexpected guests and it never fails to win compliments! And like most curries, it can also be prepared a day ahead – the taste certainly improves with keeping.

Preparation: 15 minutes
Cooking: 25 minutes

3 tablespoons oil
1 onion, sliced
A
2 cloves garlic, sliced
2.5 cm ginger, shredded
1 teaspoon mustard seeds
2 sprigs curry leaves
2 tablespoons fish curry powder combined 2 tablespoons water
2 cups coconut milk, from ½ grated coconut
1 brinjal, roll-cut into small pieces
2 tomatoes, quartered
1 can (425 g) sardines with tomato sauce
1 red chilli, sliced
1 green chilli, sliced
1½ teaspoons salt
1 tablespoon lime juice or lemon juice

Heat oil in a *kuali* and fry onion until transparent. Add **A** and stir fry until fragrant. Add curry paste and fry over low heat for 2 minutes. Add brinjals and stir fry for a further 2 minutes. Pour in coconut milk and simmer until brinjals are soft. Add tomatoes, then the sardines. Break up the whole sardines into smaller pieces with a wooden spoon. When curry comes to a boil, lower heat and simmer for 5 minutes. Add salt, red and green chillies and lastly stir in lime or lemon juice.

Serve with rice, *Paratha* (p 150), *Puri* (p 155) or *Chapati* (p 152).

Brinjal Curry

Preparation: 15 minutes
Cooking: 25 minutes

600 g brinjal, cut into 1 cm slices or roll-cut
1 teaspoon turmeric powder
½ teaspoon salt
¼ teaspoon pepper
3 tablespoons oil
6 shallots, sliced
4 cloves garlic, sliced
A
2 fresh red chilles, split into two
2 green chillies, split into two
1 teaspoon mustard seeds
3 sprigs curry leaves
1 teaspoon salt
1 cup coconut milk, from ½ grated coconut
1 tablespoon coriander powder (p 43)
250 g medium-sized prawns, shelled and deveined (optional)

30 g chopped dried prawns can also be used instead of fresh prawns. Fry with shallots and garlic until fragrant.

Marinate brinjals with turmeric powder, salt and pepper.

Heat oil in a saucepan and lightly brown shallots and garlic. Add **A** and fry until fragrant. Add salt and coconut milk and bring to a boil stirring occasionally. Add brinjals and simmer till soft. Stir in coriander powder and if using, put in prawns. Cook for a further 5 minutes. Remove and serve with *Puri* (p 155), *Paratha* (p 150) or rice.

Brinjal Puree

Preparation: 15 minutes
Cooking: 40 minutes

3 tablespoons oil or ghee

A
2 onions, finely diced
1 clove garlic, finely chopped
2 cm ginger, finely chopped

B
½ teaspoon ground turmeric
1 teaspoon chilli powder
2 teaspoons salt
1 teaspoon garam masala or your favourite curry powder

500 g brinjals, peeled and diced
300 g tomatoes, diced
½ cup water or fresh chicken stock

Heat oil in a saucepan and fry **A** until lightly browned. Add **B** and fry for 2 minutes. Add brinjals and tomatoes and cook over low heat for 5 minutes stirring occasionally to prevent vegetables sticking to pan. Add water or chicken stock, cover the saucepan and cook until vegetable becomes a thick paste. Serve with *Chapati* (p 152), *Puri* (p 155) or *Paratha* (p 150).

Garam Masala

Garam masala is a mixture of spices for Indian curries. There are many combinations. and with the addition of chillies and pepper, they become spicy and fragrant.

This recipe is fragrant and sweetish. If you require it hot and spicy, a teaspoon of chilli powder can be added to the dish. *Garam masala* can also be substituted with your favourite curry powder.

15 g cinnamon
2 level teaspoons cardamon seeds without the pods
1 teaspoon cloves
¼ piece nutmeg

Roast the above spices in a moderately hot oven until fragrant or pan-roast separately. Grind in an electric blender until very fine. Store in an air-tight container. Keeps well for months in the refrigerator.

Spicy Potato and Tomato Curry

Preparation: 15 minutes
Cooking: 25 minutes

250 g potatoes, boiled with the skin, peeled and cut into 1½ cm cubes

A
½ tablespoon chilli powder
½ tablespoon coriander powder (p 43)
½ teaspoon turmeric powder
½ teaspoon ground pepper
1 tablespoon yoghurt

2 tablespoons ghee or oil
1 onion, sliced
1 clove garlic, sliced
2 cm ginger, shredded
½ cup water or fresh chicken stock
1 teaspoon salt
1 tablespoon tomato puree
250 g tomatoes, cut into wedges
2 sprigs coriander leaves (p 43), chopped
2 sprigs mint leaves, chopped

Mix potato with **A**. Leave aside.

Heat oil in a saucepan and fry onion until transparent and soft. Add garlic and ginger and fry until fragrant. Add potatoes and fry for 2-3 minutes. Next, add water or chicken stock, salt and tomato puree. When it begins to boil, add tomatoes and simmer for 10 minutes over low heat. Just before dishing out, sprinkle in coriander and mint leaves. Serve with *Chapati* (p 152), *Puri* (p 155) or rice.

Yoghurt

Freshly made yoghurt will keep well in the refrigerator for four days without turning too sour. If you do not have yoghurt to start with, buy a carton of natural yoghurt from your local supermarket or ask your Indian neighbours for some.

Preparation: 1 minute
Cooking: 5 minutes

250 ml fresh or reconstituted milk
2 teaspoons natural yoghurt

Bring milk to a boil. Cool to lukewarm, and then drop in natural yoghurt. Cover and leave overnight at room temperature. The next day, when yoghurt is set, keep refrigerated.

Potato and Pea Curry

You will be surprised how this dish of simple ingredients can be so tasty!

Preparation: 15 minutes
Cooking: 20 minutes

250 g potatoes, cut into small (pea-size) cubes
2 tablespoons ghee or cooking oil
1 onion, diced

A
2.5 cm ginger, chopped
1 clove garlic, chopped
1 teaspoon ground turmeric
1 teaspoon chilli powder

1 cup water or fresh chicken stock (p 24)
³/₄ teaspoon salt

B
125 g frozen peas
³/₄ tablespoon garam masala (p 169) or your favourite curry powder
4 sprigs coriander leaves (p 43), chopped

Soak the potatoes in a little salt water and keep aside.

Heat oil in a saucepan and fry onion until transparent. Add **A** and fry until fragrant. Drain and add potatoes and fry for 2 minutes. Add water or stock and salt and simmer, covered, until soft. Add **B**. Cook for a further 5 minutes until gravy is slightly thick. Serve with *Puri* (p 155), *Chapati* (p 152), *Paratha* (p 150) or rice.

Mixed Vegetable Curry

Mildly spiced, this is a delightful vegetable curry that even children will enjoy.

Preparation: 15 minutes
Cooking: 20 minutes

3 tablespoons oil

A
1 medium-sized carrot, roll-cut or diced
1 potato, cut into small cubes
125 g cauliflower, cut into small pieces

2 onions, sliced

B
½ teaspoon mustard seeds
3 stalks curry leaves
2 cloves garlic, chopped
2.5 cm ginger, chopped
1 teaspoon ground turmeric

125 g French beans, cut into 2-3 sections
125 g cabbage, cut into small pieces
1 cup water or chicken stock (p 24)

C
2 tomatoes, quartered
1 teaspoon chilli powder
1 teaspoon curry powder
1 teaspoon garam masala *(p 169)*
1 teaspoon salt

2 sprigs coriander leaves (p 43), chopped

Heat oil until hot and deep fry **A** for 10 seconds. Drain and leave aside. Remove oil leaving 3 tablespoons in the saucepan. Fry the onion until soft and transparent. Add **B** and stir fry until fragrant. Add the fried vegetables, French beans and cabbage and fry for 1 minute. Pour in water or chicken stock. When it comes to a boil, add **C**. Cover and simmer for 10 minutes over low heat until vegetables are soft. Sprinkle in coriander leaves. Serve with *Puri* (p 155), *Chapati* (p 152) or rice.

Sothi

A must when serving String Hoppers, is this rich fragrant coconut milk vegetable curry delicately spiced with loads of gravy. I never seem to have enough rice when this is prepared.

Preparation: 30 minutes
Cooking: 30 minutes

1 cup thick coconut milk and
2½ cups thin coconut milk, from 1 grated coconut

A
1 onion, ground
3 cloves garlic, ground
2.5 cm ginger, ground
1 onion, cut into wedges
2 sprigs curry leaves
1 teaspoon turmeric powder
¼ teaspoon fenugreek (p 156)
2 teaspoons salt
2 potatoes, cut into wedges
150 g ladies fingers, kept whole
150 g French beans, cut into two
4 cabbage leaves, cut into squares
3 red chillies, coarsely sliced
3 green chillies, coarsely sliced

250 g small prawns, shelled and deveined
2 tomatoes, quartered
1 tablespoon lime juice

Put thin coconut milk in a cooking pot. Add **A** and bring to a slow boil. When vegetables are half-cooked, add prawns and tomatoes. Simmer till vegetables are soft, stirring occasionally. Add thick coconut milk, gently stirring to prevent curdling. When curry boils again, add lime juice and remove from heat. Serve with rice, String-Hoppers (p 158) or *Puri* (p 155).

Kabuli

Preparation: 30 minutes
Cooking: 30 minutes

Gram or *channa dhal* is the largest type of lentil. It's also sold as flour in packets in Indian provision stores.

600 g channa dhal (kacang kuda putih)
1 teaspoon salt
2 tablespoons oil
A
3 large onions, minced
1 clove garlic, minced
4 cm piece ginger, minced
B
½ teaspoon ground saffron (p 161)
1 tablespoon ground chilli
1 dessertspoon cummin, toasted and ground
1 tablespoon tamarind, mixed with a little water
salt to taste

Soak *dhal* overnight. Cook in a pressure cooker for 10 minutes with water and salt. Remove and mash coarsely with a spoon.

Heat oil in a *kuali*. Fry **A** till lightly brown. Add *dhal* and **B**. Lastly, stir in strained tamarind juice. Let it boil and add salt to taste. Serve with *Puri* (p 155).

Dhal Curry

To sweeten and flavour the curry, chop bony parts of chicken into small pieces and boil together with *dhal*.

Preparation: 20 minutes
Cooking: 45 minutes

2 tablespoons oil

A
2 onions, sliced
3 cloves garlic, sliced
2.5 cm ginger, chopped

4 teaspoons curry powder for vegetables or fish and 1 teaspoon turmeric powder, mixed into a paste with a little water
180 g dhal, washed and soaked overnight
4 ½ cups water
2½ teaspoons salt
1 brinjal, cut slantingly into small pieces
1 potato, cut into small cubes

Heat oil in a saucepan and lightly brown **A**. Add turmeric and curry powder paste and stir well over low heat. Add *dhal* and stir fry for 1 minute. Add water and salt and allow to simmer, covered for 30 minutes. Add brinjal and potato and simmer for another 10 minutes or until soft. Serve with *Paratha* (p 150) or rice.

Coconut Sambal

Preparation: 10 minutes
Cooking: 10 minutes

Sambals
These *sambals* can be served with *Thosais* (p 156-158), *Puri* (p 155), rice or simply used as a dip.

A
approximately 180 g or ¹/₂ grated young white coconut
1 teaspoon roasted dhal
3 green chillies
2 slices ginger
2 tablespoons yoghurt (p 170)
1¹/₄ teaspoons salt
1³/₄ cups water
2 tablespoons oil

B
¹/₂ teaspoon mustard seeds
1 sprig curry leaves
2 dried chillies (p 94), soaked and cut into ¹/₂ cm pieces

Put **A** into an electric blender and grind to a smooth paste. Heat oil in a saucepan and stir fry **B**. Pour paste in and simmer for 5 minutes. Remove and serve with *Thosai* (p 156-158).

Onion Sambal

Preparation: 10 minutes
Cooking: 12 minutes

4 tablespoons oil

A
4 onions, ground
8 dried chillies (p 94), ground or 1 dessertspoon cili giling
¼ teaspoon fenugreek (p 156)

30 g ikan bilis, *rinsed (optional)*
2 tablespoons lime juice
2 teaspoons sugar
½ teaspoon salt

Heat oil in a *kuali* and fry **A** over low heat until oil separates. Add *ikan bilis*, if using, and stir fry for a few minutes. Stir in lime juice, sugar and salt. Serve with *Paratha* (p 150), *Thosai* (p 156-158) or *Puri* (p 155) or as a dip.

A Deepavali feast: (clockwise from top right)
Special Chicken Curry (p 166), *Sothi* (p 173),
Idiyappum (p 158), Mutton Curry (p 166), Potato
and Plain *Puri*s (p 155).

Sugar & Spice: (in tray, clockwise from top right)
Nankathai (p 196), *Gajjah Ki Halwa* (p 197), *Muruku*
(p 180), *Kesari* (p 195) and (in centre) Mixture (p 183);
(front, far left) Sugee Gift Cake (p 205) and *Laddu* (p 193).

SUGAR & SPICE

The Festival of Lights

Deepavali or *Diwali*, as it is known in North India, is probably the single most important festival for Hindus the world over. There are various myths to explain the festival and these vary throughout India. For some, the festival signifies the beginning of the reign of Lord Rama. In South India, and for most Singaporean and Malaysian Hindus, *Deepavali* is celebrated to commemorate the destruction of the demon Narakasura by Lord Krishna. And in Northern India, *Diwali* marks the beginning of the new year, calculated according to the calendar of the Vikram era, and commemorates the reign of King Vikramaditya.

Being a religious festival, food served should be vegetarian but this is not the normal practice for the majority. Weeks before the day, kitchens will be abuzz with preprations making the various titbits that must be served to guests – it just will not be *Deepavali* without *muruku!* Various curries will be cooked on the day itself with the favourite meats being chicken and mutton. And for dessert, there will always be sweetmeats, colourful and tasty.

Muruku mould – also used for String Hoppers (p 158) and **Omapody** (p 183).

Ajowan

Ajowan is a small annual of the parsley family, closely related to cummin and caraway with the flavour of thyme – really! It's used as a spice in parts of the Middle East, Asia and especially in their native India.

Ajowan seeds (*omam*) are easily available from Indian provision stores. They keep well for a long period in an air-tight container. Use sparingly as it has a very pungent and slightly acrid flavour.

Muruku

This is something that almost all Indian homes will serve for *Deepavali* and Christmas. You don't have to wait for a special occasion (nor be Indian!) to make these three different versions of *muruku*. You'll be surprised how easy it is to make.

The *muruku* can be piped into 7½ cm lengths using a cookie press fitted with a three-star nozzle. This is less time consuming than coiling each *muruku* into rings.

Preparation: 20 minutes
Cooking: 45 minutes
Makes: enough to fill a large milk can (almost always how
        it is stored)

480 g rice flour

A
1 teaspoon cummin
1 teaspoon ajowan seeds (omam)
1½ teaspoons salt
1 teaspoon baking powder

30 g butter, softened at room temperature
3-4 cups coconut milk, from 1 grated coconut
oil for deep frying

Sift and roast rice flour in a *kuali* over low heat for 5 minutes, stirring constantly. Take care not to brown it. Otherwise, the *muruku* will have too dark a colour and taste burnt. Remove from heat and let flour cool completely, preferably overnight.

Add **A** to flour. Lastly, add butter. Gradually pour in enough coconut milk to make a stiff dough.

Heat oil in a *kuali*. Put dough in a cookie press fitted with either a one- or three-star nozzle and pipe 7½ cm lengths of dough into hot oil. (This will take longer to cook but is easier to control.) Or, pipe 7½ cm circles starting from the centre onto squares of greaseproof paper or newspaper. Press the tail end of the dough against the side of the coil of dough. This will prevent *muruku* from uncoiling when it is fried. When all the dough is used up, heat oil for deep frying until hot.

Fry over medium heat until golden brown. Drain on absorbent paper. When cool, store in an air-tight container.

Muruku with Sesame Seeds

I love this because of the sesame seeds which give it an extra fragrant nutty flavour. The recipe uses a mixture of blackgram and rice flour which makes a softer texture *muruku* than a mixture of gram dhal flour and rice flour or *muruku* using only rice flour as the first recipe.

Preparation: 30 minutes
Cooking: 30 minutes
Makes: approximately 50

180 g blackgram flour, pan-roasted
180 g rice flour, pan-roasted
¾ teaspoon salt
15 g sesame seeds, washed, drained and pan-roasted
1 teaspoon ajowan seeds (omam, p 180), washed, drained and pan-roasted
2 ¼ cups coconut milk, from 1 grated coconut
30 g margarine, room temperature

Sift roasted blackgram and rice flours into a mixing bowl. Stir in salt, sesame and ajowan seeds.

Bring coconut milk to a boil and gradually add to mixture to form a firm biscuit texture dough.

Put enough dough to fill a *muruku* mould fitted with a star nozzle and follow method as for first recipe.

If blackgram flour is not available, wash and pan roast, the same quantity of blackgram without skin. Grind in an electric pepper or coffee grinder. To ensure that it is very fine, pass through a sieve.

Muruku with Green Bean Flour

Delicately crunchy.

Preparation: 30 minutes
Cooking: 30 minutes
Makes: enough to fill half a large milk can

¾ cup coconut milk, from ½ grated coconut, mixed with ½ teaspoon turmeric powder and ½ teaspoon salt
½ tablespoon cornoil
240 g rice flour
15 g roasted green bean flour (paspaer)
1½ teaspoon ajowan seeds (omam, p 180)
1 teaspoon cummin

Green bean flour is available from Chinese and Indian provision stores. Sift the flour and pan-roast. Or, you can make your own flour. Buy unskinned green/mung beans. Wash and dry them in the sun. Roast in a dry pan before sending to the mill for grinding.

Put coconut milk, turmeric powder and salt into a pot and bring to a slow boil. Add cornoil to half a cup of this mixture. Leave aside.

Sift rice and green bean flours into a mixing bowl. Stir in ajowan seeds and cummin. Add coconut milk mixture and mix with a wooden spoon. Form and knead into a soft biscuit dough.

Fill a *muruku* mould fitted with a star-nozzle with enough dough and follow method as for first recipe.

Omapody

I have not met anybody who can resist this lovely, crunchy titbit which is excellent with beer.

Preparation: 10 minutes
Cooking: 30 minutes

90 g rice flour
105 g gram dhal flour (p 174)
½ teaspoon salt
¾ cup water, approximate

Sift rice and *gram dhal* flours into a mixing bowl. Add salt and enough water to mix to a soft dough.

Heat oil in a *kuali* for deep frying. Fill *omapody* mould (p 180 – bigger holes than that for string hoppers) with a little of the dough. Press into hot oil in a circular motion. Fry until crisp and light golden in colour. Drain on absorbent paper. Break into smaller pieces when cooled and store in an air-tight container.

Mixture

This very oddly named snack can also be served with drinks. No one seems to be able to give an Indian name for this and I'm not sure where or how this wonderful 'mixture' was created. You can get the various ingredients from Indian provision stores.

Preparation: 10 minutes
Cooking: 30 minutes

Follow the recipe for *Omapody*.

Divide the dough into two portions. Use one portion to make *omapody* with *omapody* mould (p 180) and the other portion to make finer *omapody* with mould used for string hoppers. Break into smaller pieces.

While the *omapody* is still hot mix with the following:

60 g roasted peanuts
60 g roasted green coloured *channa dhal* (p 174)
60 g roasted red-coloured *channa dhal* (p 174)
2 sprigs curry leaves, washed and dried

Store in an air-tight container when cooled.

Indian snacks:
(from top) *Vadai* (p 185),
Pakoras (p 188), Fried
Kacang Kuda (p 189),
Masala Vadai (p 186) and
Ulundu Vadai (p 187).

Vadais

Vadais are common tea-time snacks and here are my favourite recipes for three different types.

Preparation: 20 minutes
Frying: 10 minutes
Makes: 15

---

180 g dhal, *washed and soaked*

A
⅓ cup water
1 green chilli, finely sliced
1 red chilli, finely sliced
1 sprig curry leaves, finely sliced
1 teaspoon chilli powder
½ teaspoon salt

oil for deep frying

This first version has a finer texture and the fragrance of the curry leaves is more pronounced.

Soak *dhal* overnight. Drain and put into a blender with water and blend coarsely. Mix the coarsely blended *dhal* with **A**.

Heat oil for deep frying. Cut a piece of plastic sheet approximately 15 cm square. Take a walnut-size round of dough and place on the plastic sheet. Flatten slightly to form a flat round cake. Drop it into hot oil with the aid of the plastic sheet to keep *vadai* in shape. Repeat until all the dough is used up. Fry until golden in colour. Drain on absorbent paper.

Masala Vadai

This version has a crunchier texture as the dhal is coarsely pounded. The prawns give it a 'sweeter' flavour.

Preparation: 30 minutes
Frying: 10 minutes
Makes: 12

120 g dhal

A
60 g peeled small prawns, chopped
60 g shallots, finely chopped
1 red chilli, finely chopped
1 green chilli, finely chopped
1 sprig curry leaves, chopped
1 teaspoon curry powder
¼ teaspoon salt

1 egg yolk
plain flour for coating
oil for deep frying

Wash and soak *dhal* overnight. Rinse, drain and pound coarsely. Add **A** and mix well. Bind with egg yolk. With floured hands, shape into small walnut-size balls, flatten slightly and roll in flour.

Heat oil until hot in a *kuali*. Reduce heat a little and deep fry until golden brown. Drain on absorbent paper.

Ulundu Vadai

Indian doughnuts that are simply delicious.

Preparation: 30 minutes
Frying: 10 minutes
Makes: 15

180 g blackgram dhal, *without skin (p 157)*
⅓ cup water

A
1 medium-sized onion, finely diced
1 green chilli, finely sliced
1 red chilli, finely sliced
1 sprig curry leaves, chopped
½ teaspoon salt
1½ tablespoons flour
oil for deep frying

Wash and soak blackgram *dhal* overnight. Drain and put into a blender with water and blend until fine. Mix *dhal* paste with **A**. Dough will be very soft and sticky.

Heat oil for deep frying until hot. Cut a piece of plastic approximately 15 cm square. Take a walnut-size lump of dough and place on the plastic sheet. Lightly flatten and make a finger dent in the centre right through the dough to form a doughnut shape. Drop 'doughnut' *vadai* into the hot oil with the aid of the plastic sheet. This will prevent the soft dough from getting out of shape. Deep fry until golden in colour on both sides. Drain on absorbent paper.

The blender may not turn very easily because very little water is used. Do not add any liqiud but turn off the blender every now and then and stir with a teaspoon or chopstick.

Bhajia

Fritters that are great anytime of the day.

Preparation: 15 minutes
Frying: 30 minutes
Makes: approximately 25

125 g gram dhal *flour (p 174)*
¾ *teaspoon baking powder*
½ *teaspoon salt*
1 *egg, lightly beaten*
1½ *cups water, approximate*
1 *medium-sized onion, finely chopped*
3 *green chillies, finely chopped*

Sift *gram dhal* flour and baking powder into a mixing bowl. Add salt. Make a well in the centre of the flour and add beaten egg. Mix into a thick batter with water. Stir in onion and green chillies.

Heat oil for deep frying. Drop a level dessertspoon of batter into hot oil. Reduce heat to moderate and fry *bhajia* until golden brown. Drain on absorbent paper and serve hot.

That excellent and by all Physitians approved China drink, called by the Chineans Tcha, by other nations Tay, alias Tee, is sold at the Cophee House . . .

First tea advertisement in the London newspaper *Weekly News* in (1606) And with that, tea was introduced to the world. Right up till 1830, all the tea drunk in the West came from China, despite the fact tea plants were found growing wild in Assam, India in 1823. By the 1860s, this was no more true with thousands of British sailing east in the 'tea rush' with the hope of making their fortune. Now the world had English Breakfast, Darjeeling, Assam, Ceylon, et cetera. Life was never the same . . .

Pakora

Another fritter but spicier and lighter than *bhajia*.

Preparation: 15 minutes
Cooking: 30 minutes
Makes: 20

150 g gram dhal *flour (p 174)*
¼ *teaspoon bicarbonate of soda*
A
½ *teaspoon salt*
2 *medium-sized onions, diced*
4 *dried chillies (p 94), rinsed and sliced*
3 *sprigs curry leaves, chopped*
½ *cup water*

Sift *gram dhal* flour and bicarbonate of soda into a mixing bowl. Mix in **A**. Add water and mix into a soft sticky dough.

Heat oil for deep frying. Using the fingers, pinch walnut-size balls of dough and drop into hot oil. Fry until golden brown in colour. Drain on absorbent paper.

Fried Kacang Kuda

Richer version of just Boiled *Kacang Kuda*. It makes a great snack for drinks or any other time.

Preparation: 15 minutes
Cooking: 1 hour

4 tablespoons oil

A
2 cloves garlic, minced
2.5 cm ginger, minced
1 sprig curry leaves

2 teaspoons chilli powder
½ teaspoon turmeric powder
3 medium-sized onions, sliced
3 red chillies, coarsely cut
2 small tomatoes, cut into wedges
½ teaspoon salt
300 g boiled kacang kuda (garbanzo beans)
1 tablespoon lemon or lime juice

Heat oil in a *kuali* and lightly brown **A**. Put in chilli and turmeric powder and stir fry for 1 minute. Sprinkle with a little water to prevent burning. Add onions, chillies and tomatoes and fry for 3 minutes. Add salt and *kacang kuda*. Stir fry for 3-5 minutes and lastly add lemon or lime juice. Serve.

Boiled Kacang Kuda

Tea-time, anytime snack which kids especially love.

The *kacang kuda* can also be boiled in an electric rice pot. Just add water to 2.5 cm above the beans, as you would do for rice.

Preparation: 10 minutes
Cooking: 40 minutes

300 g whole *kacang kuda* (garbanzo beans), washed and soaked overnight
2½ cups water
½ teaspoon salt

Put *kacang kuda* in a pot with water and salt, cover and bring to a boil. Cook until tender and almost splitting. Remove from heat and drain well. Serve.

Samosa

Great for tea or cocktail parties, this is one of the most popular of Indian savouries which is a lightly-fried batter enclosing a meat or vegetable filling. To suit English taste, it underwent modifications to become the ever-popular 'curry puff'.

Preparation: 1 hour
Cooking: 15 minutes
Frying: 15 minutes
Makes: 16

1 tablespoon oil
2 onions, finely diced

A
1 clove garlic, minced
1 cm piece ginger, minced
½ tablespoon salt

250 g beef, minced, mixed with 1 tablespoon meat curry powder and 2 tablespoons water
½ teaspoon garam masala *(p 169)*
1 tablespoon lime or lemon juice
2 sprigs coriander leaves (p 43), chopped

180 g plain flour
½ teaspoon salt
30 g butter
½ cup water

oil for deep frying

Spring-roll skins can be used instead of making your own pastry. Cut each sheet into 4 squares. Put in filling, brush edges with water, then fold and seal into triangles.

Heat oil in a *kuali* and fry onion until transparent. Add **A** and fry until fragrant. Add meat and stir fry for 2 minutes before adding water and *garam masala*. Cook until meat is soft. Stir in lime or lemon juice and lastly coriander leaves. When meat mixture is dry, remove from *kuali*. Cool before using as filling.

Sift flour into a bowl and add salt. Blend butter into the flour, then mix into a soft firm dough with water. Knead for 5 minutes until smooth. Leave to rest for 30 minutes.

Divide into 8 portions and shape into round balls. Roll into flat thin circles on lightly floured board. Cut each circle into half. Put a teaspoonsful of filling on one end of semi-circle. Brush edges with water and fold into a triangle. Press edges together to seal.

Deep fry in hot oil until golden brown on both sides. Serve with mint chutney.

Mawa Samoosa

This is a sweet variation of the popular tea-time snack of *samosa*.

Preparation: 30 minutes
Cooking: 10 minutes
Makes: 12

A
480 g sugar
1 cup water
¼ teaspoon rose essence
3 cardamons, split open
240 g plain flour
pinch of salt
½ cup water
250 g unsweetened mawa
oil for deep frying

Bring **A** to a boil until a thick mixture is obtained. Keep syrup in a cool place.

Sift flour into a bowl and add salt. Add water and knead into a soft dough. Form into walnut-size balls and roll out into thin circular shapes. Place 2 tablespoons of *mawa* in centre. Brush edges with water and fold into half to seal filling.

Deep fry in hot oil until golden brown. Dip into warm syrup and remove immediately. Decorate with some chopped almonds and, if available, press a smaller sliver of edible tin foil on top. Serve hot.

Mint Chutney

Preparation: 10 minutes

A
1 small onion
¾ cm piece ginger
5 cloves garlic
10 sprigs mint leaves
30 sprigs coriander leaves
juice from 1 large lime
salt to taste

Finely mince **A** and stir in lime juice and salt to taste. Keep in an air-tight container and refrigerate. Serve with *samosas* or any fried dish.

Unsweetened *mawa* is made from boiling fresh milk and can be bought from Indian restaurants and small eating shops.

Edible tin foil, expensive and not very commonly used, is availabe from Indian provision stores and is used for food decoration.

Gulab Jamun

Gulab means 'rose' and this Northern Indian dessert has a predominantly rose essence. It will definitely thrill all sugar-lovers but frighten away calorie counters. Use ghee as it gives the dessert a richer flavour.

Preparation: 15 minutes
Cooking: 20 minutes
Makes: 20

A
600 g sugar
4 cups water
120 g self-raising flour
480 g full-cream milk powder
2 tablespoons ghee
6 tablespoons evaporated milk, approximate
ghee or cornoil for frying

In a saucepan, combine **A** and boil until sugar is dissolved.

Sift self-raising flour and milk powder into a large bowl. Rub in ghee, then enough evaporated milk to give a firm but pliable dough. Form into small round balls.

Deep fry in ghee or cornoil over low heat until dark golden in colour.

Remove *gulab jamun* and place them in prepared syrup in a covered container. Allow to cool completely and serve at room temperature or chilled.

Laddu

A delightful sweet popular with Northern Indians that's served at celebrations such as weddings and prayer ceremonies.

Preparation: 30 minutes
Cooking: 30 minutes
Makes: approximately 10 golf ball-sized sweets

A
240 g sugar
2 cups water
3 cardamons, split
2-3 drops orange colouring
120 g gram dhal flour (p 174)
1 cup water
¼ teaspoon bicarbonate of soda
ghee or oil for deep frying
2 tablespoons coarsely ground almonds and pistachio nuts
desiccated coconut

Perforated ladle ideal for draining oil and for making *laddu*.

Mix **A** and boil for approximately 20-25 minutes until a thick mixture is obtained. Leave aside.

Sift *gram dhal* flour into a mixing bowl and mix into a runny batter with water. Stir in bicarbonate of soda.

Heat ghee for deep frying in a *kuali* until hot. Place a flat perforated ladle with ½ cm size holes over the hot oil. Pour a little of the batter into ladle. Move in a circular motion and let droplets of batter fall into the hot oil. Stir until droplets turn light golden in colour. Remove with a clean perforated ladle and drain on absorbent paper. Repeat procedure until all the batter is used up. Put all the *laddu* into prepared hot syrup and soak for 15 minutes. Drain soaked *laddu* from syrup.

Put the drained *laddu* into a mixing bowl and mix well with ground almonds and pistachio nuts. Take a handful of the mixture and mould into firm golf ball-sized sweets. Roll and coat with desiccated coconut.

Keeps well in the refrigerator for at least two weeks.

Payasam

Indian pudding also known as *kheer* – rice *kheer*, semolina *kheer*, vermicelli *kheer* or sago *kheer* which is this recipe. The different versions depend on the occasion or what region of India the person comes from.

Preparation: 20 minutes
Cooking: 25 minutes
Serves: 6 persons

150 g sago
3½ cups boiling water
3-4 drops yellow colouring
2½ cups coconut milk, obtained from 1 grated coconut
3-4 drops yellow colouring
2 dessertspoons ghee
30 g fine vermicelli, broken into 15 cm lengths
30 g raisins
8 cashewnuts
210 g sugar
¼ teaspoon salt
¼ teaspoon vanilla essence

Wash sago in a colander. Drain and put in a cooking pot with boiling water. Cook for 5 minutes until sago turns transparent. Pour in coconut milk and continue stirring for 10 minutes. Stir in yellow colouring and remove from heat. Leave aside.

Heat ghee in a *kuali* and quick fry vermicelli until light brown. Drain with a slotted spoon and add to sago. Add raisins and cashew nuts and quick fry for 5 seconds. Pour into sago mixture. Return pot to heat again. Stir in sugar, salt and vanilla essence. When mixture comes to a boil, remove from heat. Serve hot or cold.

Kesari

Two versions of this sweet dessert which has a grainy, nutty bite of semolina.

Preparation: 10 minutes
Cooking: 30 minutes
Makes: approximately 20 pieces

A
120 g semolina, roasted
3 tablespoon water
120 g sugar
3 cardamons, skinned and finely grind the seeds
pinch of salt
1½ tablespoons ghee
30 g fried raisins
30 g roasted cashewnuts, coarsely chopped

Put **A** into a heavy saucepan. Cook over low heat stirring occasionally until mixture leaves sides of pan. Add the fried raisins and cashewnuts and when mixture becomes a mass of dough remove from heat.

Grease a flat plate 20 cm diameter with butter and spread hot mixture into it. Cool and cut into small pieces.

Kesari with Coconut Milk

Cooked with coconut milk, this version has a cake-like texture and is sweet and rich.

Preparation: 15 minutes
Cooking: 4 minutes
Makes: approximately 12 pieces

180 g semolina, roasted
4 tablespoons ghee
30 g raisins
30 g cashewnuts, split into two
2 cups coconut milk, from ½ grated coconut
120 g sugar
¼ teaspoon salt
2 teaspoons ghee

Pan-roast semolina for 5 minutes and leave aside.

Heat ghee in a *kuali* and fry raisins and cashew nuts for 5 seconds. Add coconut milk, sugar and salt and stir until sugar dissolves. Put in roasted semolina and continue stirring until mixture turns into a mass and leaves sides of pan. Press evenly into a 15 cm x 7½ cm dish and level surface with a spoon. Spread two teaspoons of ghee and press surface down firmly. Cool and cut into squares or diamond pieces.

Nankathai

Ghee biscuits that taste like shortbread and melt in your mouth.

Preparation: 20 minutes
Baking: 20 minutes
Oven temperature: 175 °C
Makes: 28 walnut-size balls

240 g plain flour	
1/4 teaspoon bicarbonate of soda	
240 g castor sugar	
120 g ghee	
chopped almonds	

Sift flour and bicarbonate of soda into a mixing bowl. Stir in castor sugar and add ghee. Knead to form a soft dough. Form into a small walnut-size balls. Place on baking trays and press a few chopped almonds on top for decoration. Bake in moderate oven for 20 minutes.

Gajjah Ki Halwa

Gajjah means 'carrot' but *halwa* can be made from any kind of flour, nuts, fruit or vegetable. One more of the 'thousand' calorie sweets of the Indians.

Preparation: 30 minutes
Cooking: approximately 20 minutes

300 g carrots, coarsely grated
1½ cups fresh milk

A
225 g granulated sugar
1½ tablespoons ghee
1 tablespoon rose water

30 g chopped almonds
60 g sultanas
60 g roasted cashewnuts, coarsely chopped
5 cardamons, skinned

Rose water is a popular flavouring for Indian sweets. Diluted from rose petals, it's sold in dark-coloured bottles and is available from Indian provision stores. If it's not available, substitute with a few drops of rose essence.

Put carrot and milk in a heavy saucepan and cook over high heat. When liquid is reduced by half, add **A**, and continue cooking, stirring occasionally.

When sugar has dissolved, lower heat, add almonds and cook for 5 minutes. Add sultanas and continue stirring. When mixture is almost dry, add cashewnuts. Keep stirring until mixture leaves sides of pan and forms a mass. Sprinkle in cardamon seeds and remove pan from heat.

Spread mixture on a 16½ cm square baking tin or dish. Use a plastic spatula to smooth the surface. When cool cut into squares or diamond shapes.

Indian sweets: (from top)
Payasam (p 194), *Mawa*
Samoosa (p 191) and *Tosha*
(facing page).

Tosha

Served for tea and festive occasions, this is a half-cake, half-biscuit sweet enjoyed by the Sindhis. The delightful lady who taught me this recipe insisted that the dough must not be rolled on the table but kneaded one portion at a time in my hand in order to obtain the shape and texture for this dessert.

Preparation: 30 minutes
Cooking: 30 minutes
Makes: 22

250 g plain flour
¼ teaspoon bicarbonate of soda

A
1 teaspoonful yoghurt (p 170)
2 teaspoons cooking oil
½ cup water

480 g sugar
1 cup water

Sift flour and bicarbonate of soda into a mixing bowl. Make a well in the centre and add **A**. Mix into a firm dough. Form into lime-sized balls. Using the fingers of one hand, form into date shapes.

Deep fry in hot oil until golden brown. Leave to cool.

Put water and sugar into a small saucepan and boil until syrup turns thick and stringy. Turn heat off and keep stirring. Drop *tosha* into cooling syrup very quickly, as syrup will crytalize and harden when it cools.

Serve decorated with rose petals.

Party spread to delight children of all ages: (clockwise from top) Tasty Fried Noodles (p 26), Nutty Buns (p 240), Sugar Crystal Cookies (p 222) surrounded by Nutty Crisps (p 227), Banana Crumble Boats (p 237), Curry Puff (p 233), *Pie Tee* (p 7), *Kuih Lapis* (p 132), Fried *Wantan* (p 62) with chilli sauce, Coconut Sago (p 141), Egg Jelly (p 248); (centre) Rich Chocolate Cake (p 202) and Steamed Beef Balls (p 56).

CAKES AND BAKES

Chocolate Butter Cream

This rich cream is most suitable for light cakes such as sponge and chiffon or for celebration cakes that require intricate decorative piping.

500 g hard butter, cut into small pieces
360 g icing sugar and 45 g cocoa, sifted together
1 cup cold fresh milk
1 teaspoon vanilla essence

Cream cut-up cold butter until soft and creamy. Beat in combined icing sugar and cocoa a little at a time until fluffy. Beat in cold milk and vanilla essence a little at a time until light and fluffy.

Ovalette

This is a stabilizer used in baking cakes to help the eggs rise rapidly and stiffly. Stabilizers are acidic and this helps the beaten eggs to remain stable and not lose their light, airy, velvety and voluminous texture which is essential for light chiffon-textured cakes. It is like cream of tartar, which is an acid and when added to egg whites acts as a stabilizer.

Rich Chocolate Cake

An ideal cake for an extra special high tea like a children's birthday party. If baking a smaller cake, use half of the recipe and bake in two 18 cm square cake pans. Decorate with choclate butter cream or chocolate icing (p 215).

A stiff batter consistency is essential for light, airy, soft chiffon-textured cakes. To achieve this, measure all the other ingredients first, taking the eggs and cold water out of the refrigerator only when you're ready to turn on your electric whisk. The cold eggs combined with commercial stabilizers such as Ovalette, help the eggs to rise more rapidly and become voluminously stiff, just what you need for a light cake. If the stabilizer is omitted, the cake will flop and not rise.

Preparation: 30 minutes
Baking: 12 minutes
Oven setting: 175°C

200 g castor sugar
200 g plain flour and 1 teaspoon double action baking powder, sifted together
6 large cold eggs
2 cold egg yolks
1 dessertspoon Ovalette or any other commercial stabilizer
1/3 cup cold water
2/5 cup melted butter, cooled and 30 g cocoa, blended
1 teaspoonful chocolate paste (p 213)
1 teaspoon vanilla essence

Put sifted ingredients into a large bowl. Add eggs, egg yolks, Ovalette and cold water. Beat at high speed for 5-10 minutes until well-risen and light.

Fold in butter mixture, chocolate paste and vanilla essence. Turn mixture into two 25 cm x 30 cm cake pans with the base lined with greased greaseproof paper. Bake in moderately hot oven for 12-15 minutes or until cooked through.

Cool and sandwich with chocolate butter cream. Decorate with grated chocolate shavings.

Traditional Sugee (Semolina) Cake

A traditional recipe that is a *Deepavali* must. Here are two variations that can be served for special occasions such as *Hari Raya* and Christmas. If using half the recipe, bake in a 11.5 cm x 22.5 cm loaf/cake tin. Use extra egg whites to make Cornflake Coconut Macaroons (p 226).

Preparation: 30 minutes
Baking: 1 hour
Oven setting: 175 °C

300 g butter
300 g sugar
½ cup milk
300 g semolina
14 medium-sized egg yolks
4 egg whites

A
120 g ground almonds
60 g plain flour, ½ teaspoon bicarbonate of soda and ½ teaspoon baking powder, sifted
pinch of salt

2 dessertspoons brandy
2 teaspoons vanilla essence

Cream butter and 200 g of sugar until light and fluffy. Add milk a little at a time. Beat in semolina and allow mixture to stand for 1 hour.

Whisk egg yolks with remaining sugar until stiff and light lemon in colour. Add to butter mixture a little at a time, beating well with each addition.

Whisk eggs whites until stiff and carefully fold into butter mixture. Fold in **A**. Beat in brandy and vanilla essence.

Pour mixture into a 25 cm square cake tin lined with double sheet of greased greaseproof paper. Bake in moderate oven for approximately 1 hour to 1 hour 10 minutes until golden in colour or until cooked when tested with a skewer.

Nutty Fruity Sugee Cake

A variation of the traditional recipe that makes an unusual Christmas fruit cake.

Preparation: 45 minutes
Baking: 1 hour 10 minutes
Oven setting: 175 °C

480 g butter
210 g castor sugar
300 g semolina, toasted and cooled
15 egg yolks
1/2 cup milk
5 tablespoons brandy
2 teaspoons vanilla essence
1/4 teaspoon rose essence

A
15 red cherries, chopped
60 g preserved winter melon, finely chopped
30 g cornflakes, crushed
30 g mixed peel, finely chopped
120 g chopped almonds
90 g plain flour, 1/2 teaspoon bicarbonate of soda and 1/2 teaspoon baking powder, sifted together
pinch of salt
1/2 teaspoon nutmeg

4 egg whites
120 g castor sugar

Cream butter and sugar until light and fluffy. Beat in semolina and allow mixture to stand for 1 hour. Beat in egg yolks one at a time. Add milk, brandy, vanilla and rose essences. Fold in **A**. Mix well. Whisk egg whites together with castor sugar until just stiff. Fold into egg yolk mixture.

Spoon mixture into a 25 cm square cake tin lined with a double layer of greased greaseproof paper. Bake in a moderate oven for 1 hour 10 minutes or until cooked through and golden in colour.

If you're not sure of the heat intensity of the top of the oven, it is always better to put in a swiss roll cake tin on the top shelf. And if the top of the cake tends to brown too quickly, place a similar cake tin on the top shelf of the oven to cover the cake.

Sugee Gift Cake

This is is a beautiful cake to make during the festive season. It keeps well for at least a month and tastes better with keeping. Cake should be wrapped in tin foil. If extra brandy is preferred, add 1-2 tablespoons to cake after 3 days. Wrap and store in a cool place.

Preparation: 45 minutes
Baking: 1 hour
Oven setting: 175°C

90 g sultanas, chopped
90 g raisins, chopped
60 g cherries, chopped
45 g mixed peel, chopped
30 g currants, chopped
60 g roasted cashewnuts, coarsely chopped
45 g ground almonds
¾ teaspoon rose essence
¾ teaspoon vanilla essence
½ teaspoon almond essence
½ teaspoon lemon essence
6 tablespoons brandy
½ tablespoon plain flour

Prepare fruits at least a day before baking. This way the essences are nicely infused into the fruits. Mix chopped fruits with cashew nuts, ground almonds and the four essences. Stir to mix well and pour in brandy. Mix again and stir in flour. Leave in an air-tight container.

150 g semolina
150 g butter
7 egg yolks
150 g icing sugar, sifted
¾ teaspoon mixed spice
2 egg whites

Roast semolina in a pan for 5 minutes. This gives it an added nutty fragrance and a crunchier and nuttier bite. Mix in butter and leave to cool for 5-6 hours or overnight.

On baking day, whisk egg yolks until light. Gradually beat in icing sugar until thick but not stiff. Fold in semolina and butter mixture and mixed spice. Add marinated fruit and nut mixture. Mix well.

Whisk egg whites until stiff. Fold in sufficient egg white to cake mix to give a dropping consistency. It may not be necessary to use up all the egg whites.

Pour into a 10 cm x 17.5 cm cake tin lined with greased greaseproof paper. Bake in a moderate oven for 1 hour to 1 hour 10 minutes.

Fruity and Fruitsie Cake

Another festive season favourite. It keeps well for one to two weeks if kept in an airtight container.

Preparation: 30 minutes (plus 12 hours for soaking fruit)
Baking: 50 minutes
Oven setting: 175 °C

A
360 g raisins
240 g currants
120 g glace cherries, quartered
120 g chopped nuts
120 g mixed peel, cut into smaller pieces
1 tablespoon brown sugar
4–5 tablespoons rum

B
300 g plain flour
1 teaspoon baking powder
1 teaspoon mixed spice
1 teaspoon ground nutmeg
¼ teaspoon salt
250 g butter
6 eggs
240 g soft brown sugar
2-3 tablespoons rum

Soak **A** in 4-5 tablespoons rum for at least 12 hours in an airtight container. Sift **B** together.

On baking day, grease and line a 22-25 cm square tin with double sheets of greased greaseproof paper.

Cream butter and sugar until light and beat in eggs one at a time. Stir in fruits. Add sifted flour, spices and salt.

Pour into prepared tin and bake for 50 minutes to 1 hour or until skewer comes out clean when inserted. While still warm, spoon over 2-3 tablespoons rum. Leave aside till cold.

Turn out cake without removing greaseproof paper and wrap in foil or a polythene bag for a day before cutting. This keeps the cake moist and traps the flavour of the rum. The cake can be cut into pieces and wrapped in coloured cellophane paper.

Golden Fruit Cake

A very simple and quick-to-make fruit cake that does not compromise on taste. The method of slow baking keeps the rich fruit cake moist. Tin foil is used to line the cake tin as it helps to cook the cake at a reduced temperature and after baking it's easier to wrap to keep it air-tight for storing. Greaseproof paper can be used for storing but then this has to be sealed completely with sticky tape.

Preparation: 30 minutes
Baking: 2 hours
Oven setting: 150 °C

1 packet (375 g) mixed fruits, finely chopped
300 g butter
300 g soft brown sugar
1 dessertspoon golden syrup
2 teaspoons grated orange rind
5 eggs
300 g plain flour
3 dessertspoons brandy

Line a 21 cm square tin with greased tin foil. Cream butter, soft brown sugar and golden syrup until light and fluffy. Beat in orange rind. Add eggs one at a time beating well after each addition. Fold in flour alternately with fruits. Bake in slow oven for 2 to 2¼ hours or until skewer inserted into the centre comes out clean.

Carefully drizzle in brandy while still hot.

If the bottom heating element of your oven is too intense, the base of the cake will be too browned. To prevent this, a layer of newspaper can be cut to line the base of the cake tin before lining with tin foil. If the top heating element or grill is exposed, place a baking tray on the top shelf, before putting in the cake to prevent the cake surface from turning too brown.

Two different pandan chiffon cake recipes. The 'Never-Fail' recipe produces a light cake with a compact texture. The *Santan* Chiffon Cake is more airy and moist.

Santan Chiffon Cake

A richer variation of the first recipe.

Preparation: 30 minutes
Baking: 1 hour 15 minutes
Oven setting: 165°C

6 egg yolks
300 g sugar
¼ teaspoon salt
1 cup thick coconut milk, from 1 grated coconut
1 tablespoon pandan juice
a few drops green colouring
240 g plain flour and 3 teaspoons baking powder, sifted twice
6 egg whites
½ teaspoon cream of tartar
1 dessertspoon cornoil

Beat egg yolks with sugar and salt till white and creamy. Add coconut milk, pandan juice and colouring. Sift in flour and baking powder and fold in lightly but quickly.

Whisk egg whites with cream of tartar until soft peaks form. Pour egg yolk mixture into egg whites and mix lightly and evenly. Stir in cornoil.

Pour batter into a well-greased 25 cm x 9 cm tube pan and bake in a moderately slow oven for 1 hour 15 minutes. Invert on a wire rack straight away and remove tin after 5 minutes.

'Never-Fail' Pandan Chiffon Cake

This has been successfully tested by friends who had never baked a cake before. They just read the recipe at least five times over before starting, making sure they had everything correct.

Preparation: 30 minutes
Baking: 45 minutes
Oven setting: 175°C

7 large egg whites
150 g castor sugar
½ teaspoon cream of tartar
7 egg yolks
150 g castor sugar

A
6 tablespoons cornoil
¼ teaspoon cream of tartar
2 tablespoons pandan juice (p 114)
1 teaspoon vanilla essence
½ cup thick coconut milk, from ½ grated coconut

150 g self-raising flour

Whisk egg whites, sugar and cream of tartar in an electric mixer until stiff and mixture holds its shape.

In a separate bowl, whisk egg yolks and sugar until light and creamy. Stir in **A**. Sift in self-raising flour and fold gently. Pour egg yolk mixture into egg white mixture and carefully mix gently and evenly.

Pour into an ungreased 23 cm tube pan and bake in a moderate oven for 45-50 minutes until lightly browned on surface. Remove from the oven and invert mould immediately. Allow to cool thoroughly before removing from pan.

Orange and Lime Chiffon Cake

A light cake that will delight your tea guests. The flavour of the orange rind and sharp tartness of the lime makes this a very welcome change from the usual *'lemak'* and rich taste of cakes such as the *Santan* Chiffon Cake. It's also less sweet.

Preparation: 15 minutes
Baking: 40 minutes
Oven setting: 175°C

4 large eggs, separated
150 g castor sugar
120 g self-raising flour and 30 g cornflour, sifted
A
grated rind of 2 oranges
juice of 2 large local limes mixed with water to make ⅓ cup
¼ cup cornoil
1 teaspoon vanilla essence

Whisk egg whites in electric mixer until soft peaks form. Add 90 g of castor sugar gradually and whisk until just stiff.

Sift self-raising flour and cornflour into separate bowl, add remaining sugar and **A**. Whisk until mixture is smooth. Add beaten egg whites. Fold mixture together lightly using a spatula.

Pour mixture into a 20 cm ungreased tube pan. Bake on centre shelf of moderate oven for 40 minutes or until cake is well browned and firm to touch. Remove from oven and invert pan immediately. Leave undisturbed until completely cold. To remove cake from pan, run a knife around sides and base of pan.

Cakes galore: (clockwise from left) Lemon Dream Cake
(facing page), Upside Down Date and Cashewnut Cake
(p 216), Layered Mocha cake (p 213), Cinnamon Pumpkin
Cake (p 215) and Banana and Coconut-Topped Cake (p 214).

Lemon Dream Cake

Whipped up in less than an hour but the result is a grand cream cake complete with topping. Good for unexpected tea guests.

Preparation: 50 minutes-1 hour
Baking: 15 minutes
Oven setting: 175°C

---

200 g plain flour, 30 g cornflour and
1 teaspoon double action baking powder, sifted

A

200 g sugar

6 large cold eggs

2 cold egg yolks

⅓ cup cold water

1 dessertspoon Ovalette (p 202)

⅖ cup melted butter, cooled

2 teaspoons lemon essence

---

1 can lemon pie filling

Put the sifted flours into a large mixing bowl. Add **A**. Whisk at high speed for 6-10 minutes until light and pale in colour. Fold in butter and lemon essence. Mix well.

Divide mixture into two 25 cm square cake tins with the base lined with greased greaseproof paper. Bake for 15 minutes until golden or cooked through when tested with a skewer.

Sandwich with lemon butter cream and top with lemon pie filling. Decorate with more lemon butter cream as desired.

Lemon Butter Cream

500 g cold butter, cut into small pieces
360 g icing sugar, sifted
1¼ cup cold milk
2 teaspoons lemon essence

Place cold cut-up butter into a mixing bowl and beat on medium speed until soft and creamy. Beat in sifted icing sugar a little at a time until soft and creamy. Pour in cold milk a little at a time. Continue beating until fluffy and light. Beat in lemon essence last. Use as desired.

Jelly-Layered Gateau

An unusual looking cake that blends east with west.

Preparation: 1 hour
Baking: 10 minutes
Oven setting: 175 °C

Optima is a special blend of cake flour with sugar already added. That's why it shouldn't be sifted. It's easily available from specialist bakery and cake shops and supermarkets.

3 large cold eggs
175 g Optima flour, unsifted
½ teaspoonful Ovalette (p 202)
1 tablespoon melted butter
½ teaspoon vanilla essence
75 g granulated sugar
½ packet (5 g) instant agar *powder (white)*
⁴/₅ cup water
½ teaspoon vanilla essence
½ cup thick coconut milk, from ½ grated coconut
1 tablespoon milk
pinch of salt
2 egg whites
50 g sugar

A
120 g granulated sugar
½ packet (5 g) instant agar *powder*
2 cups water
a few drops green colouring
3-4 pandan leaves, knotted

Line the base of a 25 cm square cake pan with greased greaseproof paper.

Whisk eggs, flour and Ovalette at high speed until light and thick. Stir in melted butter and vanilla essence.

Pour into prepared baking pan and bake in preheated oven for 10-12 minutes or until cooked through.

Put sugar, instant *agar* powder and water in a small saucepan and bring to a boil. Add vanilla essence, coconut milk, milk and salt. Stir well.

Whisk egg whites and sugar until just stiff. Pour in agar mixture and continue to whisk until well-blended. Pour mixture over cake. Chill in refrigerator.

Place **A** in a saucepan and bring to a boil. Remove pandan leaves and allow to cool a little. Pour over white jelly layer. Let jelly set in the refrigerator until ready to serve.

Layered Mocha Cake

If you want a smaller cake, use half the recipe and bake in two 20 cm cake tins.

Preparation: 1 hour
Baking: 15 minutes
Oven setting: 175°C

A
480 g Optima flour (p 212), unsifted
1 tablespoon Ovalette (p 202)
10 large cold eggs
180 g soft butter, room temperature
1 teaspoon vanilla essence
¾ cup chilled coconut milk, from 1 grated coconut;
or alternatively use 1 packet (60 g) instant coconut cream powder,
add cold water to make ¾ cup thick coconut milk
1 level tablespoon chocolate emulco or chocolate paste and
1 level tablespoon coffee paste, blended

Place **A** into a large bowl and whisk with electric mixer on high speed until light and fluffy.

In a separate bowl, beat butter and vanilla essence until creamy. Add chilled coconut milk a little at a time until well blended. Fold into egg mixture with a metal spoon.

Divide mixture into two portions. Add blended chocolate and coffee pastes into one portion, leaving the other plain. Pour mocha-flavoured portion into two 25 cm square cake pans lined with greased greaseproof paper. Bake in moderate oven for 15 minutes or until cooked through when tested with a skewer.

Repeat procedure with plain mixture.

Turn out all 4 layers of cake onto wire racks to cool. Sandwich with butter cream, alternating mocha and plain layers. Decorate as desired.

Butter Cream

500 g cold butter, cut into cubes
180 g icing sugar, sifted
⅝ cup cold fresh milk blended well with
1 teaspoon vanilla essence or 2 teaspoons instant coffee

Cut cold butter into small cubes and place in electric mixer. Beat until soft and creamy. Add icing sugar a little at a time and continue beating. When mixture is soft and light, add cold milk a little at a time and finally beat in vanilla essence. Use as required.

Chocolate emulco, chocolate and coffee pastes can be bought from specialist bakery and cake shops. They are used to give the deep rich colour normally found in commercial cakes. Alternatively, you can substitute the chocolate emulco with 15 g cocoa mixed with 1 tablespoon melted butter and the coffee paste with 1 dessertspoon instant coffee mixed with ½ tablespoon melted butter. Use these mixtures immediately.

Banana Coconut-Topped Cake

A special cake – rich and creamy with a soft texture and nutty flavour that's excellent for tea or dessert, especially if decorated with whipped cream. The added richness of the coconut topping turns an almost ordinary banana cake into a classic one that will continuously delight family and friends.

I prefer to use *pisang rastali* or ripe green bananas but any kind of ripe banana can be used.

Preparation: 20 minutes
Baking: 30 minutes
Grilling: 2 minutes
Oven setting: 190 °C

240 g self-raising flour, 1 teaspoon baking powder and 1 teaspoon bicarbonate of soda, sifted
3/4 teaspoon salt
240 g castor sugar
240 g butter, room temperature

A
1/3 cup milk
1 cup mashed ripe bananas
2 eggs
1/2 cup chopped nuts
1 teaspoon vanilla essence

Topping
120 g butter, room temperature
150 g brown sugar
90 g desiccated coconut
1 1/2 tablespoons milk

2-3 bananas, peeled and sliced

Put sifted ingredients into a large bowl. Stir in salt and castor sugar. Blend in butter with a pastry blender.

Mix together **A**. Stir into dry ingredients and beat until well-blended.

Pour batter into a 27 cm square pan lined with greased greaseproof paper. Bake in moderately hot oven for 30 minutes or until cooked when tested with a skewer.

Cream butter and brown sugar for topping until light and fluffy. Stir in desiccated coconut and beat in milk.

Remove cake from oven and immediately arrange sliced bananas to cover surface of cake. Cover cake evenly with coconut topping. Grill in preheated moderate grill for 2-3 minutes until top is lightly browned.

Cinnamon Pumpkin Cake

A Canadian friend, watching me make a pumpkin dessert, reminisced about her Ukranian grandmother's beautiful pumpkin cake. When I asked her for a recipe, all she could tell me was that it was a simple butter cake with a little bit of honey, orange rind, mashed pumpkin and 'a bit of this and that'. After three attempts, I came up with this version, which she pronounced very close to her grandmother's cake. Maybe our pumpkins taste different . . . !

Preparation: 30 minutes
Baking: 40 minutes
Oven setting: 175°C

250 g butter
210 g castor sugar
grated rind of 2 oranges
2 tablespoons honey
2 eggs
360 g cold mashed pumpkin

A
300 g plain flour
60 g custard powder
1¹/₂ teaspoons bicarbonate of soda
4 teaspoons baking powder
2 teaspoons cinnamon powder

Cream butter, sugar and orange rind until light and fluffy. Beat in honey. Add eggs, one at a time and beat well. Add cold pumpkin and beat until well-combined. Sift **A** and carefully fold in half at a time.

Spread into a 28 cm square cake tin lined with greased greaseproof paper. Bake in preheated moderate oven for 40 minutes or until skewer comes out clean when inserted.

Stand 10-15 minutes in tin before turning on to wire rack to cool. When cold, spread with chocolate icing.

You can decorate the cake with chocolate icing, chocolate butter cream (p 202), melted chocolate bars or simply dust the cake with icing sugar or icing sugar mixed with cocoa powder. To make an attractive pattern, place a paper doily over the cake and sift the sugar liberally over the cake. Remove the doily carefully.

Chocolate Icing

This is like glace icing. It's sweet and hardens with a glossy surface.

210 g icing sugar and 45 g cocoa, sifted
15 g butter
3 tablespoons milk

Combine all above ingredients in the top compartment of a double saucepan over simmering water. Stir until icing is smooth and of spreading consistency. Use immediately.

Upside Down Date and Cashewnut Cake

Surprise family and friends with this unusual cake that is quick and easy to bake.

Preparation: 30 minutes
Baking: 25 minutes
Oven setting: 175 °C

12 dates, pitted and chopped
60 g brown sugar
1 tablespoon custard powder
2 tablespoons milk
1 egg, beaten
60 g cashewnuts, chopped
150 g butter
125 g castor sugar
1 teaspoon vanilla essence
2 large eggs
120 g self-raising flour
2 tablespoons milk

Combine dates, brown sugar and custard powder. Stir in milk. Cook over low heat stirring continuously until thickened. Cool. Stir in beaten egg and cashewnuts. Spread evenly over base of 20 cm ring cake tin, lined with greased greaseproof paper.

Cream butter, sugar and vanilla essence until light and fluffy. Add eggs one at a time beating well with each addition. Fold in sifted flour and stir in milk. Spread cake mixture over date and cashewnut mixture. Bake in a moderate oven for 25 minutes or until cooked through when tested with a skewer.

Rich Indonesian Layer Cake

A must for *Hari Raya* and for the Peranakans for the Chinese New Year. This is a traditional recipe that is very rich using 15 egg yolks. For an easier recipe, see the second one.

Preparation: 20 minutes
Grilling: 1 hour
Oven setting: 175°C

6 egg whites
1 teaspoon vanilla essence
250 g icing sugar, sifted
15 egg yolks
390 g butter, softened at room temperature and beaten
120 g plain flour
½ teaspoon baking powder
2 teaspoons mixed spice

Whisk egg whites and vanilla essence until soft peaks form. Slowly add icing sugar a little at a time and continue beating until stiff. Beat in egg yolks one at a time. Continue beating, adding butter. Sift flour and baking powder half at a time into beaten egg mixture. Carefully stir until well-mixed.

Divide mixture into 2 equal portions and add mixed spice into one portion. Grease the base and sides of a 20 cm square cake tin and line base with greased greaseproof paper. Heat grill to moderate and place tin under grill for 1 minute. Remove from grill and put in a ladle of unspiced batter. Spread batter evenly by tilting tin and grill for 5 minutes. Put in ladle of spiced mixture and grill for 5 minutes.

Repeat procedure alternating non-spiced and spiced layers until all the batter is used up. Turn out and cool on a wire rack. Cut into thin slices to serve.

Indonesian Layer Cake

An easier recipe with short-cuts which makes use of only 7 egg yolks and whites.

7 egg yolks
150 g sugar
1 teaspoon vanilla essence
150 g butter, softened at room temperature and beaten
1 tablespoon brandy
90 g plain flour and
¼ teaspoon mixed spice, sifted
7 egg whites

Grease the base and sides of a 17 cm square cake tin and line base with greased greaseproof paper.

Whisk egg yolks with sugar and vanilla essence until creamy. Beat in butter and brandy, and stir in flour and mixed spice.

Whisk egg whites until just stiff. Pour egg yolk mixture into egg whites and fold gently.

Heat grill to moderate and place the prepared tin under grill for 1 minute. Remove from grill and put in a ladleful of batter. Spread batter evenly by tilting tin and grill for 5 minutes, or till lightly brown. Repeat till batter is used up. Turn out and cool on a wire rack. Cut into thin slices to serve.

COOKIES, PASTRIES & BREADS

(Clockwise): Ginger Cookies (p 225),
Nut Fingers (p 220), Cornflake
Crunchies (p 221), Sesame Cookies
(facing page), Cashewnut Rounds
(facing page) and Cornflake Coconut
Macaroons (p 216).

Cashewnut Rounds

There's no need to grease the trays when baking these cookies as there's enough oil in the dough and the cookies won't stick to the trays.

Preparation: 30 minutes
Baking: 15 minutes
Oven setting: 175°C
Makes: 62

240 g butter
120 g sugar
1 teaspoon vanilla essence
pinch of salt
120 g ground cashewnuts
150 g self-raising flour and 120 g plain flour, sifted together
16-20 cherries, quartered

Cream butter and sugar together until smooth. Add vanilla essence and salt, then stir in ground cashewnuts and sifted ingredients. Mix well.

Shape teaspoonfuls of the mixture into balls and press a cherry quarter into the centre. Place on ungreased trays and bake in a moderate oven for 15 minutes until golden. Cool on trays.

Sesame Cookies

Preparation: 40 minutes
Baking: 15 minutes
Oven setting: 175°C
Makes: 50

180 g butter or vegetable shortening
180 g castor sugar
1 egg yolk
¼ teaspoon salt
1 teaspoon lemon essence
120 g plain flour and 120 g self-raising flour, sifted together
1 tablespoon milk
1 cup sesame seeds, washed and toasted in the oven

Cream shortening and sugar and beat in egg yolk till creamy. Add salt and lemon essence. Gradually fold in sifted flour and stir in milk.

(cont'd on p 220)

Shape teaspoonfuls of the mixture into small balls and roll in sesame seeds. Place on greased trays and bake in a preheated moderate oven for 15-20 minutes.

Nut Fingers

A great favourite with children. These cookies will keep fresh longer if the jam is omitted.

Preparation: 1 hour
Baking: 20 minutes
Oven setting: 175 °C
Makes: 24 pairs

210 g plain flour
2 teaspoons baking powder
A
90 g castor sugar
³/₄ teaspoon vanilla essence
pinch of salt
1 egg yolk
¹/₂ egg white (reserve remaining half for glazing)
105 g cold butter, cut into small cubes
nuts for decoration
strawberry or any other favourite jam

Sift flour and baking powder into a mixing bowl. Add **A**. Stir well to mix. Add butter and blend with pastry cutter or knife. Work with fingers to form into a ball of soft pastry.

Roll out pastry on a floured board over a plastic sheet into a rectangle 3 mm thick. Cut into 1 cm x 10 cm fingers. Carefully lift fingers with a flat-bladed knife onto well-greased trays. Brush with remaining egg white and decorate with nuts. Bake in a moderate oven for 20 minutes or till golden brown. Cool and sandwich with jam. Store in an air-tight container.

Alternatively, dip both ends of the cookies into melted chocolate. Allow to dry before storing in air-tight containers or in the refrigerator.

Cornflake Crunchies

A quick and simple recipe making use of ingredients normally found in a kitchen.

Preparation: 30 minutes
Baking: 12 minutes
Oven setting: 175°C
Makes: 34

105 g butter
120 g sugar
1 egg yolk
90 g self-raising flour
30 g plain flour
180 g raisins
cornflakes, crushed lightly

Cream butter and sugar until light and fluffy. Beat in egg yolk. Sift in dry ingredients and mix well, then stir in raisins. Roll teaspoonfuls of the mixture in lightly crushed cornflakes. Place on greased oven trays and bake in a moderate oven for 12-15 minutes.

Chequered Biscuits

This takes a little extra time to make but it's worth the effort as it's bound to draw admiration from your guests.

Preparation: 45 minutes
Baking: 15 minutes
Oven setting: 175°C
Makes: 35

A
250 g or 1 block (250 g) butter, room temperature
75 g icing sugar, sifted
75 g castor sugar
pinch of salt
1 teaspoon vanilla essence
420 g plain flour
15 g cocoa, sifted
1 egg white, beaten

(cont'd on p 222)

Cream **A** until light and fluffy. Add sifted flour to form a soft dough. Remove one third of the dough (approximately 360 g). Roll in between polythene sheets into 10 cm width and 1.25 cm thick rectangle. Leave in the freezer for 30 minutes.

Knead cocoa into the remaining plain dough. Remove 360 g of cocoa dough and roll into the same size rectangle as the plain dough. Place in the freezer for 30 minutes. Wrap remaining chocolate dough in a polythene bag and leave in the refrigerator.

Remove the plain and chocolate doughs from the freezer and cut each into five 2 cm long strips. Assemble the five plain and four of the chocolate strips into a chequerboard design, brushing and sealing with a little beaten egg white.

Combine remaining chocolate strip of dough with remaining chocolate dough and roll out thinly between polythene sheets to a 10 cm width rectangle, large enough to wrap around the assembled strips of dough. Seal with beaten egg white, chill in the refrigerator for 30 minutes until firm.

• Cut the dough into 5 mm thick slices, place on well-greased baking trays and bake in a moderate oven for 15 minutes. Remove the biscuits with a palette knife and cool on wire racks.

Sugar Crystal Cookies

For special occasions, stamp the dough into different shapes. I particularly like the star shape.

Preparation: 30 minutes
Baking: 15 minutes
Oven setting: 190 °C
Makes: 60

250 g butter
135 g castor sugar
1 egg
480 g plain flour,
1½ teaspoons baking powder and ½ teaspoon salt, sifted
1 egg white, lightly beaten to glaze
¼ teaspoon ground cinnamon and 60 g granulated sugar, combined

Cream butter and sugar until light and fluffy. Add egg and beat well.

Sift flour and baking powder and add salt. Carefully stir into butter mixture.

Take a small portion of dough at a time and roll out on a lightly floured board to a thickness of 3 mm. Stamp into 6 cm circles and place on greased baking trays.

Brush with beaten egg white and sprinkle generously with combined cinnamon and sugar. Bake in a preheated moderately hot oven for 15 minutes until light golden in colour. Cool on wire racks and store in an air-tight container.

Featherlite Jam Cookies

These cookies literally melt in your mouth. If you run short of cornflour, increase the plain flour to 540 g.

Preparation: 45 minutes
Baking: 20 minutes
Oven setting: 175 °C
Makes: 160-170

240 g margarine
180 g butter
180 g icing sugar, sifted
grated rind of 3 oranges
2 teaspoons vanilla essence
480 g plain flour and 30 g cornflour, sifted together
3 teaspoons baking powder
strawberry or any other favourite jam

Cream margarine and butter together with sifted icing sugar until light and creamy. Beat in orange rind and vanilla essence. Add sifted flour and mix with a spatula until combined, then beat with electric mixer until smooth. Grease baking trays and set oven to moderate.

Put mixture into a cookie press or icing tube fitted with a star nozzle. Pipe in circles starting from the centre, leaving a small hollow in the centre. Fill each hollow with ¼ teaspoon of strawberry or any other favourite jam.

(cont'd on p 224)

Bake in a moderate oven for 20 minutes or until pale golden in colour. Cool and store in an air-tight container.

Vanilla Swirls

The golden sugar crystals are an attractive decoration and also give a crunchier bite. You can also sprinkle the cookies with chopped nuts instead of using sugar.

Preparation: 45 minutes
Baking: 12 minutes
Oven setting: 175 °C
Makes: 110 cookies

3 eggs
1 egg yolk
165 g icing sugar, sifted
75 g castor sugar
250 g butter, softened at room temperature
1 teaspoon vanilla essence
360 g plain flour and 2 teaspoons baking powder, sifted together
1 egg white, lightly beaten to glaze
golden sugar cyrstals or local coarse sugar to sprinkle

Cooked egg yolks are used for the mixture as it makes the cookies more fragrant and light. It's amazing what a simple variation can do.

Boil eggs for 10-12 minutes, plunge into cold water and shell. Press the hardboiled egg yolks (discard the egg whites) through a fine sieve and mix into the fresh egg yolk together wiht the sifted icing sugar and castor sugar. Gradually work in the butter and vanilla essence. Lastly, work in sifted flour and baking powder until just combined. Place in an electric mixer and beat until smooth.

Grease baking trays and set oven to moderate heat. Put mixture into a cookie press or icing tube fitted with a five-star nozzle. Pipe into rosettes starting from the outer circle. Brush centre of each cookie with beaten egg white and sprinkle with golden sugar crystals. Bake for 12 minutes or until pale golden in colour.

Ginger Cookies

Preparation: 30 minutes
Baking: 15 minutes
Oven setting: 175 °C
Makes: 70

A
5 dessertspoonfuls golden syrup
240 g margarine
210 g castor sugar
420 g plain flour
3 teaspoons ground ginger or 2 dessertspoons ginger juice (p 35)
2 teaspoons baking powder
2 teaspoons bicarbonate of soda
¼ teaspoon salt
1 egg yolk, lightly beaten

Melt **A** in a saucepan over a gentle heat. If using ginger juice, add to syrup mixture.

Sift flour, ground ginger, baking powder and bicarbonate of soda into a mixing bowl. Stir in salt. Add syrup mixture and beaten egg yolk to dry ingredients, beat well and leave covered in refrigerator overnight.

Next day, spoon out a quarter of the hardened dough. Keep remaining dough refrigerated. Roll out dough thinly on a lightly floured board and cut into 5 cm rounds or any other shape. Place in greased baking trays and bake in a moderate oven for 15 minutes until light golden brown. Repeat with rest of mixture. If the centre of the cookies are still slightly soft after baking, turn the cookies over carefully with a metal spatula and bake again for 3-5 minutes. Let stand for a few minutes, then carefully lift onto wire racks with spatula to cool completely.

Cornflake Coconut Macaroons

This recipe makes use of extra egg whites you may have from baking a cake.

Preparation: 20 minutes
Baking: 20 minutes
Oven setting: 165 °C
Makes: 100-110

4 egg whites
270 g icing sugar, sifted

A
2 teaspoons vanilla essence
180 g desiccated coconut
180 g cornflakes, lightly crushed
210 g dark chocolate, finely chopped

Whisk egg whites until soft peaks form, gradually add icing sugar and keep on whisking until mixture is of stiff meringue consistency. Add **A**. Mix thoroughly.

Using two teaspoons, shape a teaspoonful of meringue mixture into round balls and drop onto baking trays lined with greased greaseproof paper. Bake in moderately slow oven for approximately 20 minutes until firm.

Almond Butter Crisps

Preparation: 30 minutes
Baking: 15 minutes
Oven setting: 175 °C
Makes: 100

360 g butter
300 g castor sugar
2 egg yolks
1 teaspoon vanilla essence
¼ teaspoon almond essence
180 g self-raising flour
300 g plain flour

almond slices for decoration

Cream butter and sugar until light and fluffy. Beat in egg yolks, vanilla and almond essences and salt. Sift in flours and mix well.

Shape teaspoonful of the mixture into small balls and place on greased trays. Press sliced almond into the centre and bake in a moderate oven for 15 minutes until light golden in colour. Cool on wire racks.

Nutty Crisps

A quick and easy recipe if the kids want something different for tea. If you like a tangier flavour, use lemon or lime juice.

Preparation: 30 minutes
Baking: 20 minutes
Oven setting: 175°C
Makes: 20

120 g plain flour
60 g cornflour
120 g cold butter, cut into small cubes
90 g sugar
1 teaspoon orange juice and ½ egg yolk, combined
½ egg white, beaten lightly
120 g chopped nuts

Combining the orange juice with the egg yolk gives a better texture. If only orange juice is used, the dough will be too 'wet' for rolling and the cookies will be a little heavier.

Sift flour and cornflour into a mixing bowl. Put in cold butter and blend with a pastry cutter or knife. Stir in sugar and bind dough with orange juice and egg yolk mixture.

Roll dough out thinly on a lightly floured board over a plastic sheet. Cut into 6 cm circles or star-shapes (as in picture on p 201). Lift cookies onto greased trays, using a flat, broad-bladed knife. Brush with egg white and sprinkle with chopped nuts. Bake in moderate oven for 20 minutes or till golden brown. Cool and store in an air-tight container.

Pineapple Jam

Pineapple jam can be made and stored in air-tight jars in the refrigerator for at least a month.

4 cups liquidized and strained pineapple
360 g cups sugar
2-3 pandan leaves
1 teaspoon vanilla essence

Place all ingredients in a saucepan and cook over low heat, stirring constantly until jam is thick. Allow to cool. Store in jam jars and use as required.

Coconut Tartlets

Substitute the pineapple filling with coconut.

1 egg
90 g castor sugar
90 g desiccated coconut

Whisk egg and sugar and stir in coconut. Fill pastry with this filling and bake in a moderate oven for 25-30 minutes till golden brown.

Pineapple Tarts

A great favourite during festive periods – be it Chinese New Year, *Hari Raya*, *Deepavali* or Christmas. Or make your high tea an extra special one. Just follow the pineapple jam recipe and try out the four different variations to the simple tart.

Quick and Easy Pineapple Tarts

Preparation: 30 minutes
Cooking: 30 minutes
Baking: 25 minutes
Oven setting: 190 °C
Makes: 30

250 g cold butter, cut into small cubes
60 g castor sugar
1 egg yolk
pinch of salt
1 teaspoon vanilla essence
270 g plain flour, sifted

Cream butter and sugar and beat in egg yolk. Add salt and essence. Fold in sifted flour and put mixture into a cookie press fitted with a star nozzle.

Pipe in circles, starting from centre, onto greased patty tins. Fill each hollow with 1 teaspoon of jam. Bake in a moderately hot oven for 25-30 minutes till pale golden.

Transfer to a wire rack. When cool, store in an air-tight container.

Lattice Pineapple Tarts

This is a bit more time consuming to make than the other versions. But it's nice for special occasions. Your guests will be completely bowled over especially when they can't even find time to make simple things!

Preparation: 1 hour
Cooking: 30 minutes
Baking: 30 minutes
Oven setting: 175°C
Makes: 22

150 g plain flour
180 g self-raising flour
pinch of salt
165 g cold butter, cut into small pieces
1 egg, beaten
¼ cup cold water
pineapple jam (p 228)
1 egg yolk, beaten and 2 teaspoons evaporated milk, mixed and beaten for glaze

1

Sift plain and self-raising flours into a mixing bowl and add salt. Rub in butter or blend with pastry cutter. Add beaten egg and bind pastry with water.

Roll out pastry, half at a time, on a lightly floured board over a plastic sheet, to ½ cm thickness. Cut pastry with a 5 cm plain cutter and place on squares of greaseproof paper.

2

Put 1 teaspoon jam in the centre of each round of pastry. Line thin strips of pastry in a lattice over jam. Cut a ring of pastry and place around lattice. Using pastry pincers, pinch the edge of the pastry round for decoration.

Place tarts on a cookie tray and bake in a moderate oven for 25-30 minutes. Brush pastry with egg and milk glaze while still oven-hot. Cool on a wire rack and store in an air-tight container.

3

Dainty Pineapple Tarts

Preparation: 30 minutes
Cooking: 30 minutes
Baking: 15 minutes
Oven setting: 175°C
Makes: 40

120 g plain flour
120 g self-raising flour
pinch of salt
150 g cold butter, diced
1 egg yolk and 2 tablespoons ice-cold water, combined
pineapple jam (p 228), formed into lime-sized balls

Sift plain and self-raising flours into a mixing bowl. Add salt. Blend in butter with a pastry blender until mixture resembles fine breadcrumbs. Add combined egg yolk and cold water and lightly knead to form a soft dough.

Roll out pastry on a lightly floured board and stamp into 3 cm rounds with a pineapple tart mould. Fill centre with pineapple jam. If desired, flute sides with a pastry pincher. Bake in moderate oven for 15 minutes or until light golden in colour.

Various pineapple tart moulds with, pastry pinchers for fluting edges.

Pineapple-Shaped Tarts

Preparation: 1 hour
Cooking: 30 minutes
Baking: 15 minutes
Oven setting: 175°C
Makes: 50-60

250 g butter, room temperature
450 g plain flour, sifted
1 egg, lightly beaten
pinch of salt
1 tablespoon cold water
cloves

Stir butter in a mixing bowl and add flour and salt. Blend with a pastry blender. Put in beaten egg and lightly bind pastry dough with water. Cover soft dough with a tea towel.

Form into small pieces of dough the size of a walnut. Flatten each piece with the palms of your hands, dipped in flour to prevent sticking. Fill with jam and carefully shape dough into pineapple shapes. Make shallow cuts with a pair of small scissors to form pineapple patterns. Stick a piece of clove to represent the stem. Brush pineapple tarts with beaten egg and bake in a moderate oven for 15 minutes until golden.

Curry Puffs

The Indian *samosa* (p 190) modified to suit English taste and another preferred tea-time snack. Three recipes are given here – fried, puff pastry and the unique shell curry puff for special occasions. All recipes use the same filling.

Curry Puff Filling

Makes: enough for 30-35 curry puffs

240 g chicken, beef or pork, cut into small cubes
2 tablespoons meat curry powder
2 tablebspoons oil
2 onions, finely diced
2 medium-sized potatoes, cut into small cubes
1 teaspoon salt

Season meat with curry powder.

Heat oil in a *kuali* and lightly brown onions. Add potatoes and fry till almost soft, adding just enough water to prevent drying. Add meat and salt.

Stir fry till meat is cooked and dry. Dish out and let oil drain away from meat by tilting dish before filling.

Fried Curry Puffs

Preparation: 1 hour
Cooking: 15 minutes
Makes: 22

420 g plain flour
½ teaspoon salt
180 g margarine
1 egg yolk, beaten
¾ cup cold water

Sift flour into a bowl and add salt. Rub in pastry margarine with a pastry cutter until mixture resembles fine breadcrumbs. Make a well in the centre of flour mixture and add beaten egg yolk and water and mix to a soft dough. It may be necessary to add a little extra cold water.

Roll out pastry, half at a time to ¼ cm thickness and cut into 9 cm rounds.

Take a piece of cut pastry, put a dessertspoon of filling in the centre. Fold pastry into half to enclose filling. Seal by pinching and fluting the edges.

Heat oil for deep frying. When oil is hot, fry curry puffs until golden brown. Drain on absorbent paper.

Curry Puffs

This recipe uses puff pastry which can be stored in well-sealed polythene bags and frozen for as long as a month. When required, thaw out before rolling out.

Preparation: 1 hour
Cooking: 15 minutes
Baking: 25 minutes
Oven setting: 190°C
Makes: 35

180 g pastry margarine, at room temperature
480 g plain flour
1½ teaspoons baking powder
⅜ cup cornoil
1 egg, beaten
1¼ cups cold water with juice of 2 local limes and ¼ teaspoon salt
1 egg yolk, beaten and 2 teaspoons evaporated milk , mixed and beaten for glaze

You can use either lime or lemon juice. This makes the pastry 'crunchier' and crispier, as we say it more *garing*.

(cont'd on p 244)

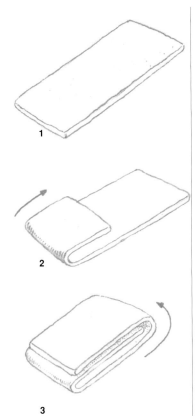

1

2

3

Roll out pastry margarine between large clean plastic sheets into a 15 cm x 20 cm rectangle. Chill in the refrigerator.

Sift flour and baking powder into a mixing bowl. Add cornoil and beaten egg and blend with a pastry cutter or knife until mixture resembles breadcrumbs. Bind with water, lime and salt mixture using a wooden spoon. Turn out and knead on a lightly floured board. Dough must be soft but not sticky.

Roll out dough into a rectangle twice as long but of the same width as pastry margarine rectangle.

Remove plastic sheets from pastry margarine and place in the centre of the rolled out dough. Fold over the dough to cover pastry margarine and seal edges. Roll out into a rectangle twice as long as it is wide and fold the two edges by overlapping, making three layers altogether. Repeat rolling and folding procedure twice. Divide pastry into two for easier handling and use as required.

Roll out one half thinly and cut into 6-7 cm strips. Cut into 7½ cm x 12½ cm rectangles and put in filling. Fold over and seal edges with a little water. Bake on ungreased trays till golden in colour. Brush with egg and milk glaze as soon as the curry puffs are removed from the oven.

Shell Curry Puffs

Binding the two pastries together makes a nice shell-like pattern, hence the name.

Prepration: 1½ hours
Cooking: 15 minutes
Makes: 20

Pastry A
300 g plain flour
3½ tablespoons lard or vegetable shortening
¼ teaspoon salt
¾ cup water

Pastry B
180 g plain flour
3½ tablespoons lard or vegetable shortening

Sift flour for **Pastry A** into a mixing bowl. Make a well in the centre and add lard, salt and water. Mix together to form a soft dough. Knead well until smooth. Cover dough with a tea towel and leave for 30 minutes.

Sift flour for **Pastry B** into a mixing bowl. Blend in lard to form a soft dough. Divide into 20 even pieces.

Roll rested **Pastry A** into a long sausage roll and cut into 20 even pieces. Flatten each piece of **Dough A** into a flat circle and place a portion of **Dough B** in the centre. Gather edges to enclose **Dough B**. Flatten again and roll out on a lightly floured board in to a small rectangular shape. Roll up like a swiss roll. Repeat this procedure again.

1

Cut each small roll into equal halves. Place cut side up and roll into a 15 cm flat circle. Put 2 teaspoons of curry meat filling in the centre of uncut side. Fold and shape into a half-moon and pinch the edges together to seal in the filling. Pleat decoratively.

Heat oil for deep frying and fry over medium heat fro 5-6 minutes or until golden in colour.

2

Chicken Pie

This is the Oriental version of the Western chicken pie. Sinking your teeth into one of these will remind you of the Hainanese cook in starched whites who used to get it just right all the time. The chicken pies that you now get in the stores use very little chicken (and that is if you're lucky!) and the filling is not as tasty. The long prepration time makes up for the final product.

Preparation: $1^1/_2$ hours
Cooking: 30 minutes
Baking: 20 minutes
Oven setting: 220 °C
Makes: 24

240 g chicken, diced
A
1 teaspoon sugar
1 teaspoon sesame oil
2 teaspoons light soya sauce
$^1/_2$ teaspoon salt
dash of pepper
1 tablespoon oil
60 g carrots, diced
120 g potatoes, diced
120 g onions, diced
90 g green peas
1 teaspoon cornflour mixed with 1 tablespoon water
1 stalk spring onion, chopped
1 sprig coriander leaves (p 43), chopped
180 g pastry margarine, at room temperature
480 g plain flour
$1^1/_2$ teaspoons baking powder
$^3/_8$ cup cornoil
1 egg, beaten
$1^1/_4$ cups cold water mixed with juice of 2 local limes and
$^1/_4$ teaspoon salt
1 egg yolk, beaten
2 teaspoons evaporated milk, mixed and beaten for glaze

Season chicken with **A**.

Heat half the oil and fry diced carrot and potato. Remove to a dish.

Heat remaining oil and fry 1 teaspoon onion till fragrant, then add chicken. When cooked, add cooked carrot and potato. Add rest of diced onion and finally peas. Stir in cornflour and water mixture. Dish out and stir in chopped spring onion and coriander. Leave aside while preparing puff pastry.

Follow method for puff pastry as for curry puffs (p 234). Roll pastry on a lightly floured board and cut into rounds with a 7½ cm fluted cutter (the size of the patty tin lid). Then, using a larger (8½ cm plain cutter, cut rounds to line the base of the patty tins.

Fill with a heaped teaspoonful of filling. Moisten edges of pastry and place lid on top. Press edges together, prick top and brush with glaze mixture. Bake in a very hot oven for 20 minutes or till golden.

Banana Crumble Boats

An easy recipe that will thrill the kids and that tastes good, too. Baked Banana Crumble Boats can be frozen for as long as two months in an air-tight container. Simply reheat in an oven toaster when the crowds descend.

Preparation: 1 hour
Baking: 40 minutes
Oven setting: 205 °C
Makes: 35

180 g pastry margarine, at room temperature
510 g plain flour
1½ teaspoons baking powder
⅜ cup cornoil
1 egg, beaten
¾ cup cold water mixed with juice of 2 small limes
180 g butter, room temperature

Pastry margarine can be rolled out in between polythene sheets ready for use and kept in the freezer for as long as 6 months.

(cont'd on p 238)

A
300 g plain flour, sifted
300 g castor sugar
½ teaspoon cinnamon powder

B
3 teaspoons sugar
1 teaspoon cinnamon powder

6-7 bananas, sliced

1 egg, lightly beaten to glaze

Roll out pastry margarine in between large clean polythene sheets into a 15 cm x 20 cm rectangle. Chill in the refrigerator.

Sift flour and baking powder into a mixing bowl. Add cornoil and beaten egg and blend with a pastry cutter or knife until mixture resembles breadcrumbs. Bind with water and lime mixture using a wooden spoon.

Turn out and knead on a lightly floured board. Dough must be soft but not sticky. Roll out dough into a rectangle twice as long but of the same width as pastry margarine rectangle.

Remove plastic sheets from pastry margarine and place in the centre of the rolled out dough. Fold over the dough to cover pastry margarine and seal edges. Roll out on lightly floured board into a reactangle twice as long as it is wide and fold into three. Repeat rolling and folding procedure twice. Divide pastry into two for easier handling and use as required.

Place butter in a mixing bowl, add **A** and cream together until mixture turns crumbly. In a separate bowl, combine **B**. Toss banana slices in this mixture until evenly coated.

Roll out one half of pastry thinly (cover the other half with a damp tea towel) and stamp into boat shapes with a cutter 5½ cm x 10½ cm. Brush with beaten egg and join two pieces together by placing another piece of pastry on top. Brush surface with beaten egg and spread two heaped teaspoons of crumble mixture evenly on surface. Top with 2 slices of banana. Bake in a hot oven for 40 minutes until topping is golden in colour.

Buns

The breadman on his motorcycle or in his van used to have a wide array of tea-time treats – coconut buns, curry buns, slices of thick banana cake. But like many good things, his 'honking' horn is slowly disappearing. Now all you need is little time in your kitchen and the old treats will be on the tea table.

Coconut / Curry Buns

Two of the most favourite at tea or as a snack. Follow the same method for the bread and just vary the filling.

Preparation: 2 hours
Cooking: 15 minutes
Baking: 15 minutes
Oven setting: 205℃
Makes: 24

1 tablespoon sugar
½ cup lukewarm water
2½ cm cube fresh yeast
360 plain flour
½ teaspoon salt
60 g butter, softened at room temperature
⅜ cup milk
1 egg yolk, beaten and
1 teaspoon evaporated milk, mixed and beaten for glaze

If fresh yeast is not available, dried yeast can be used. It works just as well and has the added advantage that it can be stored for a couple of months. 45 g fresh yeast is equivalent to 22 g dried yeast.

(cont'd on p 240)

Coconut Filling

½ **cup cornoil**
180 g plam sugar **(gula melaka),** **cut into small pieces**
1 small white coconut, **grated**
pinch of salt

Heat oil in a *kuali* and melt palm sugar over medium heat. Add grated coconut and salt and fry till evenly coated with palm syrup. Dish out and cool. Leave aside.

Curry Filling

2 tablespoons oil
2 onions liquidized or diced
2 medium-sized potatoes, **cut into small cubes**
240 g chicken, beef or pork, **cut into small cubes**
2 tablespoons curry powder
1 teaspoon salt

Season the meat with curry powder.

Heat oil in a *kuali* and lightly brown onions. Add potatoes with a little water and fry till soft. Put in seasoned meat and stir fry till cooked. Add salt. Fry till dry. Dish out and cool.

When a recipe calls for the bread dough to be kneaded, make sure this is done thoroughly to incorporate air.

Dissolve sugar in lukewarm water and drop in yeast cube. Let stand for about 15 minutes till yeast turns frothy. Make sure that liquid added to yeast is just lukewarm. If it is too hot, the rising action of the yeast will be killed.

Sift flour into a bowl and add salt. Mix in butter with a knife or blend with a pastry cutter until mixture resembles breadcrumbs. Pour in frothy yeast liquid and milk and mix with a wooden spoon, then work with hands to firm dough.

Turn dough out onto a floured board and knead until smooth. Return to bowl and cover with a damp cloth. Leave dough for about 1 hour till it is double its original bulk. Punch down and let it rise again.

Turn onto a floured board, knead and form into a long roll. Cut into 24 portions.

Shape portions into balls and roll out on lightly floured board. Put a teaspoonful of filling in the centre and fold in the edges. Seal and shape into round balls and place on greased trays well apart to allow spreading.

Leave to rise for about 10 minutes, then bake in a preheated oven for 15-20 minutes. As soon as buns are removed from the oven, brush with egg and milk glaze. Cool on a wire rack.

Nutty Buns

This is an original recipe of mine not found in the breadman's lot. The icing makes it a little grand and you can serve it at a children's birthday party or when you have guests over for tea.

Preparation: 20 minutes
Baking: 25 minutes
Oven setting: 205 °C
Makes: 12

30 g fresh yeast (p 239)
2 tablespoons lukewarm water
½ cup milk
60 g butter
30 g sugar
½ teaspoon salt
1 egg, lightly beaten
300 g plain flour
75 g butter, room temperature,
75 g brown sugar and 90 g chopped nuts, combined
1 dessertspoon butter, melted
90 g icing sugar, sifted
½ teaspoon butter
1 dessertspoon milk

Drop yeast in lukewarm water and allow to stand 5-10 minutes until frothy.

Heat milk and butter until butter melts. If milk is too hot, cool and then stir in sugar, salt and beaten egg.

Sift flour into bowl, add yeast liquid and milk mixture. Beat with electric mixer for 2-3 minutes until smooth. Cover with a clean cloth and allow to rise for 45 minutes or until doubled in bulk.

Punch down and turn on lightly floured board. Roll out dough into approximately 38 cm x 30 cm rectangle. Spread combined butter and brown sugar on dough and sprinkle 60 g of nuts over butter mixture. Roll up like a swiss roll starting with the longer side. Using a sharp knife cut into 12 equal portions. Arrange buns into a greased deep 21-22 cm round cake tin. Allow to rise for 20-30 minutes. Brush with melted butter and bake in hot oven for 25 minutes until golden brown. Turn out onto a wire rack to cool.

Combine icing sugar, butter and milk in a double saucepan over simmering water. Stir until icing sugar is smooth and 'satiny'. Using a spoon, dribble icing over surface of buns. Sprinkle with remaining chopped nuts.

When bread dough is placed in bowl for rising, make sure that the rising dough does not touch the cloth covering it, as this will retard rising.

There are several ways to give loaves a shiny finish – brush with melted butter immediately when it comes hot from the oven or brush with thick sugar syrup. Brushing with an egg white and water mixture also gives a good shiny finish and by brushing with milk or melted butter before baking, breads will have a golden, soft crust.

JELLIES

Papaya Jelly Bowl (facing page)

Papaya Jelly Bowl

An interesting dessert that's grand enough for a birthday party. The zest of the lemon peel and juice make the bland papaya taste 'zippy'. Try it and see what I mean.

Preparation: 10 Minutes
Cooking: 30 minutes

500 g papaya, skinned
grated rind of 1 lemon
1 dessertspoon lemon juice
1 packet (25 g) agar strips
4 cups water
300 g sugar
1 packet (110 g) orange jelly cystals
½ cup hot water
240 g fresh ripe papaya, skinned and cut into cubes

Blend papaya in a blender. There should be 1½ cups papaya pulp. Add lemon rind and lemon juice and slowly bring to a boil over low heat. Allow to cool.

Wash *agar* strips and boil with water and sugar, stirring constantly. When *agar* and sugar dissolve, remove from heat.

Dissolve orange jelly crystals in hot water and stir into *agar* mixture. Add papaya pulp mixture and stir until well-blended. Pour into a 21 cm jelly mould. Allow to cool a little, then add papaya cubes. Set in refrigerator and unmould before serving.

Soyabean Almond Jelly with Rambutans

You can use either fresh soyabean milk or packet soyabean milk for this recipe. However, I prefer the stuff fresh from the *tau huay chwee* stall or homemade soyabean milk as it is more fragrant. You can also substitute it with plain milk. The almond essence will then come through more strongly.

Preparation: 20 minutes
Cooking: 10 minutes

1 packet (12 g) agar *powder*
4 cups soyabean milk
120 g sugar
1 teaspoon gelatin
1 tablespoon hot water
¹/₂ cup evaporated milk
1 teaspoon almond essence
1 can (565 g) rambutans
3 maraschino cherries, halved

Dissolve *agar* powder in soyabean milk. Boil with sugar, stirring constantly. When sugar dissolves, remove from heat.

Dissolve gelatin in hot water, add to soyabean-*agar* mixture together with evaporated milk and almond essence. Pour into a mould, allow to cool, then set in the refrigerator.

Unmould onto a deep serving dish and pour rambutans over jelly. Decorate with cherry halves and serve thoroughly chilled.

Santan Agar-Agar Flan

A lovely light dessert.

Preparation: 30 minutes
Cooking: 15 minutes
Baking: 15 minutes
Oven setting: 190 °C

2 eggs
60 g castor sugar
½ teaspoon vanilla essence
60 g self-raising flour, sifted
½ tablespoon cornoil, melted butter or sunflower oil
½ tablespoon coconut milk
7 g agar *strips*
1 cup water
120 g sugar
¼ cup thick coconut milk, from ½ grated white coconut
½ teaspoon pandan or vanilla essence
1 large egg white
2 maraschino cherries, sliced
whipped cream

(cont'd on p 246)

Grease a 20 cm sponge flan tin thoroughly and coat base and sides with flour.

Whisk eggs, castor sugar and vanilla essence until thick and white. Sift in sifted flour and quickly fold into batter with a metal spoon. Stir in cornoil and milk.

Pour batter into the prepared tin and bake in a preheated moderately hot oven for 15 minutes until golden in colour. Allow to cool before turning out.

Wash *agar* strips and boil with water in a saucepan. Add sugar and stir constantly until sugar dissolves. Add coconut milk and pandan or vanilla essence. When mixture boils, remove from heat and cool slightly.

Whisk egg white until stiff. Strain jelly mixture into egg white, whisking at the same time.

After turning out cooled cake, gently pour freshly prepared filling into flan and chill. Decorate with cherries. Cover sides of cake with whipped cream and chill throughly.

Sherry and Mango Trifle

Preparation: 30 minutes
Baking: 12-15 minutes
Oven setting: 190 °C
Cooking: 10 minutes

2 eggs
60 g castor sugar
½ teaspoon lemon essence
60 g self-raising flour, sifted
½ tablespoon cornoil, melted butter or sunflower oil
½ tablespoon coconut milk

60 g custard powder
3 cups coconut milk
75 g castor sugar
½ teaspoon vanilla essence

1 (110 g) packet strawberry or cherry jelly crystals
1 cup hot water

4 tablespoons sherry
1 small can (565 g) mango slices in heavy syrup or
1 large fresh mango, sliced

reserved mango slices
jelly cubes
¼ cup whipped cream

Follow method of sponge base given for *Santan Agar-Agar* Flan (p 245) but use an 18 cm x 28 cm lamington tin instead of flan tin.

Dissolve custard powder in a little of the coconut milk. Put in a saucepan with the rest of the coconut milk, sugar and vanilla essence. Stir over low heat until mixture thickens and boils.

Carefully slice cooled sponge base into two even layers. Place one cake layer, cut side up, into a deep glass dish of about the same size. Sprinkle half the sherry over the cake. Top with mango slices, reserving a few slices for topping. Pour half the prepared custard over the mango slices. Chill in the refrigerator for 15-20 minutes to set custard.

Dissolve jelly crystals in hot water. Pour one-third of the jelly into a small flat dish and allow to set in the refrigerator. When firm, cut into cubes for topping. Allow remaining two-thirds of jelly to cool before pouring over the set custard. Chill in refrigerator until jelly sets.

(cont'd on p 248)

Place remaining cake layer, cut side down, on top and then sprinkle with remaining sherry. Pour remaining custard over the second cake layer. (If custard should thicken, add 1 tablespoon coconut milk or milk and return to low heat, stirring until smooth. Use immediately.) Allow custard to cool then refrigerate until firm.

Top with reserved mango slices, jelly cubes and whipped cream.

Egg Jelly

Preparation: 15 minutes
Cooking: 15 minutes
Makes: 24

24 empty egg shells with a small hole at one end
1 packet (25 g) agar strips
1½ cups sugar
4 cups water
1 teaspoon vanilla essence
a few drops green colouring
a few drops yellow colouring
a few drops red colouring
a few drops blue colouring

Wash and dry egg shells in the sun.

Wash *agar* strips and put in a saucepan to boil with water and sugar. Add essence. Divide melted *agar* into four bowls and add a few drops of one colour to each bowl.

Place egg shells on egg holders, open side up, and slowly fill each egg shell from a beaker. Let jelly cool and refrigerate.

Just before serving, crack egg shells and arrange on a dish.